Are You The
ONE
For Me?

Are You The ONE For Me?

How to Choose the Right Partner

John James
and
Ibis Schlesinger

Reading, Massachusetts • Menlo Park, California • New York
Don Mills, Ontario • Wokingham, England • Amsterdam • Bonn
Sydney • Singapore • Tokyo • Bogotá • Madrid
Santiago • San Juan

Library of Congress Cataloging-in-Publication Data

James, John, 1946–
　Are you the one for me?

　Bibliography: p.
　Includes index.
　　1. Mate selection.　2. Interpersonal relations.
3. Self-actualization (Psychology)　I. Schlesinger,
Ibis.　II. Title.
HQ801.J28　1987　　646.7'7　　86-26548
ISBN 0-201-14581-2

Cover design by Sally Bindari, Designworks
Text design by Kenneth J. Wilson
Set in 10-point Caledonia by Compset, Inc., Beverly, MA

ABCDEFGHI-DO-8987

Second Printing, July 1987

BCDEFGHIJ-AL-8987

To Ian, Javi, and Matt

So you will make the right choice when you're ready

Acknowledgments

We want to express the deepest of thanks to:

Muriel James. Just knowing that she was there with us through thick and thin gave us a sense of hope and positive expectation. We deeply appreciate her patience and persistence, and her willingness to share her experience as a writer and her words of advice, criticism, encouragement, and direction. Thanks for encouraging us to share more of what we know and who we are with others, not just as citizens of our country but as citizens of the world.

Sue Hughes, for coming over at any time of the day or night, even reading in her car at 2:30 A.M. by the light of a street lamp. For helping us with our grammar, for writing funny anecdotes and metaphors in the margins, and for liking each chapter as it was developing into a book. She gave us inspiration by reassuring us that what we were writing would actually be helpful to people.

Cyrisse Jaffee, our editor at Addison-Wesley, for her understanding of the topic and sharp eye at spotting strengths and gaps, and for her editorial comments and suggestions that seemed overwhelming at first but were always on target. She challenged us to write what we know. Thank you for being so clear and easy to work with and for your faith that this book would develop into an inspiring yet practical book.

Our clients, students and trainees, who have taught us so much; and our friends and family, who put up with us, took care of us, and applauded our efforts.

Thank God for people like you!

Contents

Chapter 3

MEETING THE ONE YOU'VE BEEN
WAITING FOR

Chapter 4

THE DATING GAME

Chapter 5

INTERVIEWING THE RIGHT PARTNER

Chapter 6
ROMANCE AND THE BEGINNING OF LOVE

Chapter 7
THE DYNAMICS OF CHANGE

Chapter 8

MAKING YOUR FINAL DECISION

Chapter 9

THE RIGHT RELATIONSHIP WITH THE RIGHT PARTNER

Are You The One For Me?

Introduction

If you are like most people, you don't want to spend night after night alone or go through a string of affairs to finally find that special someone who's right for you. You want information about relationships that makes sense and that you can use. You want to find a partner who is right for you *once and for all*. And you want to get on with your life. We have written this book for you!

Many people who want to be in a relationship believe it should come naturally, without a lot of thought or planning. They imagine that they will meet someone, fall in love, get married, and live happily ever after. Although this is indeed a cliché it is still often true.

Yet in today's world, this seldom happens. Too many people get into a relationship not knowing how to make sure it's really the right one for them. And then when it goes sour, they wonder where they went wrong and what they can do to make sure they don't end up in the same place again.

While counseling singles and couples about relationships over the years, we have often been asked:

"Will I ever find the right partner or am I just hoping for too much?"

"What can I do to meet the kind of person I want?"

"What can I do to find out about what someone's really like?"

"How can I know I'm not going to get hurt again?"

"Can I trust myself to make a right choice?"

"Once we're together, what can we do to make sure we stay that way?"

We have watched many of our friends, colleagues, clients, and family members struggle with their love relationships. In helping them find ways to succeed at love, we have discovered some particular principles and techniques that have helped them make the right choices and create long-lasting relationships. We have taught these ideas and techniques to many other singles and couples with a high degree of success, and we want to share them with you.

We have tested our approach in professional training seminars and workshops around the world—Europe, Central and South America, Southeast Asia, Canada, and the United States. We have found that these ideas apply to people of all ages and to people from different countries and cultures. The case examples in this book are true. The names and particulars have been changed for obvious reasons. If they sound familiar, it's because there is something universal about how people handle affairs of the heart.

Good relationships don't just happen, they are chosen and created. You can't just depend on common sense, intuition, or luck. In this book, we offer you a new and unique way of finding out quickly what a potential partner is really like and deciding wisely whether that person is really right for you. More specifically, this book will help you do five things:

1. Get clear on what you want in a loving relationship.
2. Discover the real reasons you haven't met the right partner yet.
3. Learn ways to prepare for that encounter when you do.
4. Have techniques to use to find out if the person you've met is right for you.
5. Have the tools you need to make your relationship a lifelong success.

In the first chapter we examine your dream of an ideal partner and the relationship you imagine would be right for you. In the second chapter, we look at the mind-sets you have that help or hinder your chances of finding the right partner. In the third chapter, we look at what you need to do to get ready for the right relationship and what you can do to make meeting the right partner more likely. We also examine what might be holding you back from going for your dream. In the fourth chapter, we present the common personality styles you are likely to meet, the dating games people play, and how to avoid games in favor of intimacy.

Following this essential information, in the fifth chapter we present our unique way of finding out the not so obvious things you need to know about your partner. This is to help you make the choice that's right for you. We also suggest ways you can let your partner know about you so he or she can also make a wise choice. In the sixth chapter, we look at what you may experience when you fall in love and some of the romantic pitfalls to avoid. The seventh chapter reviews the predictable stages of development that relationships go through as they mature, so you can predict the future of yours. In the eighth chapter, we present a technique for finally deciding if the person you are with is right for you. In chapter nine, we highlight the aspects of a relationship that make it last, so that you can make sure that yours continues to be right for you.

Throughout the book we have designed exercises to help you think about and use these ideas. We suggest you either use this book or a separate notebook to record your answers. Later, you might want to share these thoughts with someone you meet. If you are already in a relationship now, you can do some or all of the exercises alone or together. You will find that it is always interesting and sometimes a fun way to get to know each other better. One exercise can give you enough material to spend a whole night talking about.

The approach we suggest works: the logic behind it is straightforward, and the techniques included are easy to use. Many other people have found that the ideas and techniques in this book have worked for them, and they can work for you. It's time to take charge of your love life.

Are You The
ONE
For Me?

Chapter 1

✌✍✌✍✍

DREAMS OF
THE RIGHT PARTNER

"All my life I've had this dream. I see myself coming home from work and sitting with the person I love in front of a warm fire. In my dream I hear us laugh, I feel our love, and I see us grow old and our relationship getting deeper as time goes by.

"Then I come back to my everyday routine and wonder: Where is this person who will share my dream? I hope that person is somewhere, someplace. I know we'll find each other, but I don't know how. I keep telling myself to be patient, to keep looking, to get prepared, to persevere. I tell myself to hold on to my dream, because dreams can come true! Then I wonder, what can I do to make my dream come true?"

Most people search for the man or woman of their dreams. Although many of us wonder (and sometimes despair) whether our dreams can come true, we still think, talk, and strive for them. The dream of finding the right partner is one of the most important dreams people design for themselves.

Being with the right partner and in a loving relationship can become the foundation for achieving other aspirations. This love can become a home base that feels familiar, safe, and encouraging. It can help you recharge your inner batteries before you make your next foray into the world. Even more, once you are with the right partner, other dreams become easier to achieve because the relationship can be a continuous source of pleasure, nourishment, and encouragement.

This first chapter will introduce you to some new ideas about life dreams and show you how you can become aware of the dreams you have about finding a partner who is right for you. You will find out how such dreams originate, how to build on realistic ones, how to let go of old ones that haven't worked out, and how to develop new ones that will. If you are like most people, you probably have had some dreams come true and others not. You are probably in touch with some of your life dreams and not with others. You can bring these more subtle dreams into your awareness so that you can design a program to get the right partner. In the process, you may need to let go of painful memories or numbness due to past shattered dreams.

Life Dreams Pull Us to the Future

Life dreams are images or pictures that people create about how they want their life to be in the future. These life dreams are not the chaotic fantasy dreams that occur during a night's sleep, nor are they the wandering images of daydreams. Life dreams are the conglomerate of hopes, wishes, ideals, and goals that people have for their future life. In addition to the dream of a right partner, life dreams can include career success, financial security, a loving family, travel, fame, fortune, and much more. Any and all of these elements pieced together form a mosaic of your unique design.

Dreams may be modest or grand, vaguely defined or crystal clear, a burning passion or a quiet desire. Certain aspects of a life dream will be conscious and inviting, whereas others will be less conscious but are nonetheless guiding forces. Some aspects of life dreams are rational and rooted in reality; others are more like a magical fantasy.

Thinking about future dreams can spark imagination, determination, and action. Dreams are powerful motivators that invite people to reach for their goals and beyond. For centuries, life dreams have inspired people to go beyond the mundane. People frequently talk of ancestors who were motivated to seek a better life, such as the pioneers and immigrants who created the roots of "the American dream."[1]

To understand people, it is necessary to know what they want for the future. Life moves in a forward direction. Life dreams pull us to the future and as they do, they generate excitement and vitality.

Dreams of Love

Central to a person's life dream is the dream of being in a loving relationship. Dreams of love include specific images and elements of relationships which, when combined, form a picture—like an intricate mosaic or quilt—of a desired love life. They also include segments of favorite love stories, memories of special relationships, words of romantic songs, and fantasies of an ideal partner. The dream of being with an ideal partner in the future can be so magnetic that people make the effort to risk meeting new people.

For people to feel the magnetic pull of their dream of love, they need to be sure they want to be in a loving relationship and know their reasons for getting into one. Understanding your reasons can help build a successful and satisfying future. If your reasons are not clear, the relationship may be undermined at a later date when the real reasons surface unexpectedly.

People give a variety of reasons for wanting a relationship. These range from wanting to leave their parents' home to having someone to share their lonely nights with; from wanting to have a baby before they're too old to wanting to have someone to take care of them financially or when they're sick; from wanting to be accepted by a world that expects people to be married to wanting to have someone to be a parent to their children; from wanting a live-in maid to wanting someone to grow old with.

If you know what you want, your dream of love can serve as a beacon in the distance to use for navigating through life's storms. Then, in emotional droughts, when no one at all seems to be in sight, or when the wrong partners keep showing up, or during times of frustration with someone you thought would be the right partner but is not, the dream of an ideal partner can still remind you of what is important and worth going for.

Dreams Are Rooted in the Past

Dreams may be born out of simple curiosity, or they can originate from a need. They can be created from yearnings for something new or come from a desire to replicate positive experiences from the past. Dreams of love often form as a person wishes or desires something different from what is currently available.

Most children begin to design their relationship dreams on the basis of their experiences with their parents. For example, Ryan remembered his parents lying in bed at night reading. He would go in and snuggle up to them and listen to them chitchat about world events or personal gossip. The memory was so special he decided this was one of the things he wanted when he got married.

As Ryan got older, he became aware of relationships that had qualities that never existed in his parents' marriage. For example, he had these memories from a visit to his aunt and uncle's house: "I went to their home once for a family picnic. I still remember Uncle Bill playing on the lawn with the kids while Aunt Rosalee was on the patio talking with the other adults. What impressed me was how they looked at each other across the garden in such an affectionate way." From this experience, Ryan decided he wanted a relationship "where we can both be doing different things but still feel close to each other." This added another piece to Ryan's dream mosaic of the kind of partner and relationship he wanted.

Children also develop their images of an ideal relationship when they observe other grown-ups outside the family. A soccer or gymnastics coach, a teacher or youth leader, a family friend or other important adult, may have enormous impact on a child's developing dream. For example, Donna spoke tenderly of the unusual relationship her next-door neighbors had. "Charlie brought Loretta flowers at least once a month and they ate dinner by candlelight almost every Friday night. Even after being married for many years, they are still very romantic. I want that too."

Donna's dream continued to expand. She recalls when she was eleven years old: "One Sunday morning I went to my friend's farm and had breakfast with her family. I remember we had pancakes with bacon and eggs and orange juice. Then we just sat on the porch together talking and throwing sticks for the dog. We sat around enjoying ourselves like that for a couple of hours. Since then, I've thought of that Sunday breakfast a million times. That's my dream of an ideal family relationship." For Donna, the relaxed and comfortable sharing during family meal time constitutes an important part of her dream mosaic.

Some children grow up in difficult family situations and find great solace in reading. They read fairy tales or other stories that show life different from their own. They learn about other ways to live from these vicarious encounters and the images the characters present often become important models for their dreams of a loving relationship.

As children become teenagers, they learn more about relationships from their conversations with friends and from their dating experiences. These add important additional pieces to the dream mosaic. Robert recalls, "I was sixteen and deeply in love. We were both sure we would get married when we finished school. We used to share our dreams. We talked about where we wanted to live and even designed the home we wanted to live in. We also talked about how many children we wanted to have and what we wanted to be when we got older.

"I remember one day we both talked to an older friend. We told him we were in love and about our intentions of getting married 'someday.' He bet us twenty dollars that we would not get married. His emphatic prediction made us angry. We were willing to bet not just twenty, but forty dollars that we would be married.

"Sure enough, he was right. Our lives took different paths. My family moved out of town. Determined to keep our love alive, we wrote long and frequent letters. But as time went by the intensity of our correspondence diminished. Our love finally faded and we both found someone new. What still remains is the memories of the dreams we shared which were to come true with someone new."

As adolescents become adults they also become exposed to other realities of the world. Some question their earlier life dreams, others begin concrete planning on how to make them come true. They gather information, consider options, and plan strategies. Their planning sometimes becomes more practical and their dreams become more conscious. They may be involved in a relationship and decide to live together or get married. Or they may delay their decision or decide this person does not fit their dream at all and end the relationship.

When a previous relationship fulfills some major aspects of a person's dreams, he or she is likely to want a future relationship to have these same qualities. For example, Sara frequently remembers how patient and understanding her ex-lover was, how he always called her on time, and how they spent hours talking about their careers and other hopes for the future. Those moments were so special that she dreamed of something similar with her new partner. David thought back to how his ex-partner took care of him emotionally and satisfied him sexually. He used these memories to fuel his dream of having a new partner satisfy him in these same ways.

Exercise: **What Is Your Ideal?**

You've probably known or seen some people who seemed to be exceptionally good to their partners. Let these images come to mind. Which people have been so special that you might have wanted to find a partner with similar characteristics? For Kristin, her composite picture or mosaic was formed of memories of a friend's parents who played tennis together, an early boyfriend who was confident and assertive, a college professor who had a good sense of humor and was willing to listen to her, and her boss who treated his wife in openly affectionate ways. What images make up your mosaic?

	Who	*What was special for you about their relationship?*
From childhood: _____		
_____		
_____		
From adolescence: _____		
_____		
_____		
From adulthood: _____		
_____		
_____		
Currently: _____		
_____		
_____		
_____		
_____		

We blend many images together when creating a dream of an ideal partner: from real life examples, from movies and books, from past relationships and from the yearnings and creations of our minds. We select bits and pieces from memory and imagination. Later, we put them together. The final design may or may not make sense to other people, yet it is what we carry deep in our hearts. Dreams of an ideal partner can become so important that they exert strong influence on our decisions and actions throughout our lifetime.

As you think about these people, recall if you hoped to be in a similar relationship. Keep this in mind, as it can give you clues about the partner and the relationship you are looking for. Getting clear on the composite picture of your ideal relationship is like putting together a jigsaw puzzle; with each answer you find, the picture of what you want becomes clearer.

What Do People Want in a Partner?

What do people typically look for in a partner? Are there any common factors that seem almost universal? Some current studies throw light on the subject. One study found that the most common characteristics people listed when asked to describe what they were looking for in a mate are honesty, intelligence, a good sense of humor, and an openness to new ideas.[2] Another study showed that people also wanted someone who is stable, who likes to talk, enjoys quiet moments, has his or her own interests, enjoys going places and is willing to work on the relationship to make it succeed.[3] These are the preferred qualities most people include on their "shopping list" for a right partner.

Seemingly, there are differences between what men and women want in a relationship. Research by Carol Gilligan of Harvard University showed that women most often look for a sense of connection, whereas men typically want a relationship that allows them autonomy.[4]

Age is another factor that affects what men or women want.

According to Daniel Levinson, Gail Sheehy, Lois Davitz, and other researchers, what a man calls "the ideal mate" changes as he grows older.[5] In his 20s, a man is typically looking for a woman who is physically attractive and willing to listen to him talk about his initial career efforts without giving too much advice. In his 30s, a man tends to have a much more extensive list of preferred qualities. He wants a woman who is energetic, sympathetic, and trusting, more of a partner than a girlfriend, someone to share his thoughts, a good conversationalist and a good mother. When he enters his 40s, he may want a woman who takes care of herself physically and who is willing to experiment with new lifestyles and avoid the routine that so often develops in middle age. This woman is also expected to be affectionate, charming, and gentle. In his 50s and later life, he will tend to become more interested in someone who will be a companion and a friend and who will stand by him in a crisis.

Women's expectations and desires may be equally rigorous and change over time. In her 20s, a woman often wants a man who is intelligent, highly motivated, and fun to do things with. In her 30s, she may be more interested in someone who is solving his career crises and is ready to settle into a secure relationship and build a family. She often wants a man who will be a good father or step-father and who also treats her in a "special" way. At the same time, she may want a man who recognizes that her function in life is not limited to being housewife and mother, and who will support her in her efforts to return to school or work. In her 40s, she wants a man who is willing to break old patterns and expand ways of seeing and doing things. She often wants men to be open to listening and talking. Like men in their 50s and older, a woman of this age looks for a friend, companion, and caretaker—someone with whom she can enjoy life and its new challenges.

The following list incorporates some of the ideas of Levinson, Sheehy, Davitz, and the authors in regard to differences between what men and women want. You may have some wants similar to those mentioned and others that are different.

What Men and Women Want in a Partner

Women in their 20s

She wants a man who is dynamic, intelligent, motivated, and fun

She wants to fall in love, get married, and have a baby, or to postpone marriage and go to college

She believes in his dream and has high hopes for him

She is willing to support him in his career efforts, and his interests usually come first

She is willing to be his teacher, guide, host, critic, and sponsor

Women in their 30s

She wants him to be supportive in her career or educational efforts

She wants him to be kind, considerate, and to treat her special

She wants him to be established in his career and to make a commitment to settle down

She wants him to be a good father or step-father and to build a close family

She wants him to share the chores and responsibilities

Men in their 20s

He wants her to be physically attractive and a good sexual partner

He wants her to be nurturing, predictably affectionate, and loyal

He wants her to share his dream, to be supportive, and to believe in him

He wants to support his wife, have children, and own a nice home

He wants to be a success in his career, to be a good provider, and to give her everything she wants

Men in their 30s

He wants her to be interesting, sympathetic, trusting, and a good conversationalist

He wants her to be energetic and productive

He wants her to be independent and to make decisions for herself

He wants her to be a good mother, to take care of the kids and the house

He wants her to be available when he needs her

Women in their 40s+	Men in their 40s+
She wants him to break old patterns of seeing and doing things, and to explore and experiment with new lifestyles	He wants her to be understanding and supportive of his life changes and life crises
She wants him to be strong, young at heart, open to listening and talking	He wants her to take care of herself physically
She wants him to be passionate and a good sexual companion	He wants her to be gentle, tender, compassionate, affectionate, and loving
She wants him to be a friend, companion, and caretaker	He wants her to be charming and his intellectual companion
She wants him to enjoy life's new challenges, to share her interests, and to have quiet moments at home	He wants her to be willing to experiment with new lifestyles and to avoid routine living
She wants him to look to the future with new ideas and enthusiasm	He wants her to be a friend and companion and to stand by him in a crisis

Naturally, each person is looking for a partner with a unique combination of qualities. But people also tend to want many of the same characteristics. This list is intended to help you to become aware of what you want in a partner and how your wants may change over time.

Look at the list above. Probably the characteristics of more than one age group are appealing to you. They were for Karen, a woman in her 30s who had a short but fairly typical "shopping list." "I want my man to be available and honest. But I also want him to be interesting, kind, considerate, responsible, and willing to support me in my career. I also want him to have power, prestige, and money. I know that's a lot to hope for and I don't know if I'll find a man with all the characteristics I want, but I'll sure keep on looking." Some of Karen's requirements tend to be part of the universal qualities most people are looking for. Others are unique to her.

What's on Your Shopping List?

It can be interesting to know what "typical" people include in their list, but you're not typical—you're special. You have unique wants and desires. You may want many of the same qualities that other people are looking for, yet also have some particulars that are important for you—your own special "shopping list."

You may be looking for some qualities that others wouldn't want, while others might feel comfortable living in a situation that you would find intolerable. One person may be willing to live with a partner who travels frequently on the job, whereas you might find that kind of lifestyle upsetting. You might enjoy a partner who drinks occasionally; someone else may detest it. Another person might be glad to have a partner who isn't very interested in sex, whereas you may find that lack of interest intolerable. You may be looking for a partner who doesn't want children or for someone who is interested in having a big family.

Your "shopping list" can include traits and behaviors you may want to be sure that your partner does *not* have or do. You may want someone who doesn't argue, doesn't smoke, doesn't gossip, doesn't have big thighs, or doesn't wear glasses. Somebody else might want someone who doesn't swear, doesn't nag, doesn't have too much body hair, doesn't snore, isn't sloppy, or doesn't drive fast.

Exercise: Your Shopping List

Take some time and make up a list of what you're shopping for in a partner.

_____
_____
_____
_____
_____
_____
_____
_____

Now put a plus beside those items that are most important to you and a minus beside those which are least important. Rewrite your shopping list putting your wants in their order of priority.

_____
_____
_____
_____
_____
_____
_____
_____

The more specific and clear you can be in what you want, the more likely you are to get it—that is, if your requirements are reasonable and you don't expect the other person to be superhuman. If your requirements are too rigid, finding the right person may be a gargantuan task. Allow for some flexibility, and you'll have a good chance of finding and keeping a partner who's right for you.

Can My Dreams Come True?

Do you ever doubt that your dreams can come true? Doubts are natural and common, even when people feel sure of what they want in a partner.

Some people doubt their capacity to attract the right partner and dread the thought of finding themselves in a struggle with the wrong partner trying to make a bad situation work. Yet they do not want to live alone nor do they want to give up hope of finding the love of their life. So they put their longing for a lifelong partner in deep storage. They know their dream exists, but they keep it in hibernation until the right person shows up and they can thaw out emotionally.

Sometimes people live at such a deprived level that their thoughts focus more on survival than on future possibilities. When rejected or ignored, beaten down or kept out, they decide that good guys don't always win; those who experience the hard sides of life often think dreamers are naive. For them dreams are very hard work or just not obtainable, except as a matter of luck. They tend to think life is unchangeable and become resigned, bitter, or despairing as they cannot have what they want.

Other people doubt that the right partner actually exists. They might say "Searching for the right partner is like looking for perfection and, obviously, nobody's perfect!" Others believe that trying to find the right partner is a foolish waste of time. For example, you may think that it is over-romanticizing to imagine a Prince or Princess Charming will come along and sweep you off your feet into marital bliss. Or you may believe that anyone can learn to live with nearly anybody "if they just work at it."

Exercise: Identifying Your Questions and Doubts

What doubts do you have when you think about finding the right person to love? Have you ever heard yourself wonder:

- Will I ever be able to find the right partner?

- Will I recognize the right person when I see him or her?

- Will it be somebody I've known for years and just haven't paid attention to, or somebody I bump into unexpectedly?

- How much longer do I have to wait? Have I missed my chance?

- In the past, did I let the man or woman of my dreams slip right through my fingers?

- Will I make the right choice, or will I get fooled and end up in a bad relationship?

Jot down some of the questions and doubts you've raised:

_____

_____

_____

_____

_____

_____

_____

_____

It's useful to have questions and doubts. When you question, you will likely look for answers and this search will prepare you for a good relationship. Having doubts may keep you on your toes. Instead of being too sure of your opinions, your doubts may motivate you to put more energy into planning and going after your dreams. The questions and doubts you have can lead you to discover that it *is* possible to find the man or woman that you've been looking for!

But What About a Shattered Dream?

Depression often follows the loss of a dream. This can occur when a dream doesn't work out or when it gets shattered. Existence can seem to lose its meaning. People often stop dreaming when a relationship ends abruptly with a lover's death, or with the death of love when a partner is discovered having an affair. In the first situation, the grief is overpowering. The loss of a loved one can feel like a deep wound. It is hard to forget the emptiness. The sadness that remains can dampen the desire to try again. When one partner has had an affair, there is often a deep feeling of anger for being betrayed. People who have gone through this experience frequently mention that their dream of fidelity has been destroyed. They question whether it is smart to trust or love someone again.

When people don't allow themselves to grieve for love lost, they also do not allow themselves to dream about the future either. They may find that they have difficulty concentrating on solving problems or even in daily functioning. They may begin to feel tired, depressed, and lifeless. Or they may resign themselves to being only half alive; they function in the real world but feel numb emotionally. They may have creative explanations or excuses for why they are not making their life a success, but often their explanations become their main solace in their loneliness.

All of us slow down as a result of a broken love relationship. After a respite, most of us manage to get moving again, but some don't. They stay in the same place year after year. Without a dream or a way to live it out, life begins to lack genuine purpose and meaning.

Obviously, you can't erase memories of loss, but you can take the sting out of them by allowing yourself to grieve. An old Chinese proverb roughly translates, "You can't get from point A to point B until you're willing to leave point A." You need to let go of those painful memories to get on with your life. You need to heal. If you find you can't heal on your own, you may need to look for support and consider going for therapy.

Keep in mind that people can dream when feeling lonely, or even under more adverse conditions. Viktor Frankl, a prisoner of Nazi concentration camps and the founder of an approach to psychology called *logotherapy*, writes of the will to find meaning even when there seems to be no hope for the future. Regardless of the situation, a person can take a stand, whether positive or negative, affirming or denying. This he called "the defiant power of the human spirit," meaning that people have the capacity to resist and brave whatever condition they are in or whatever kind of conditioning they've had, whether biological, psychological, or sociological in nature. He emphasized the importance of "facing your fate without flinching" and going for your dreams with a firm sense of determination.[6]

Dreams Influence Decisions

When people know what they want, decisions become easier to understand and easier to make. You can learn to make them on the basis of whether or not your decision will bring you closer to your dream. If your goal is to meet someone who is a good dancer, you may decide to spend time and energy learning to dance. If your dream is to have a long-term relationship, you may decide to stay in a relationship that is temporarily going through a tough time rather than give up too early.

Talking about his life dreams, Jason said, "I believe that if I have a dream that is important to me it will come true. But I also know I have to be realistic about it. I've had a lot of setbacks because I originally picked the wrong partner. Now I've decided just because one relationship didn't work out doesn't mean the next one won't. I just need to work and get prepared to do something about it."

People make different decisions about going for their dreams. Some hesitate, and others dive right in and keep swimming. This is how it was for Dean and Joanne. Ever since they met, they knew they would get married. They also knew when they would buy a house and have children. They had their life all planned out and they followed their schedule. But how many people do you know that pursued their goals so single-mindedly? Probably not many.

Many people decide to take things as they come. They may not be sure of what they want to spend their life doing. They search around from one career to another, from one partner to another, thinking that if they're lucky they will find who or what they want. They may struggle to not get trapped in a mold or enslaved trying to live out someone else's dream. They may know what they *don't want* but they have little sense of what they *do want*. Therefore they only learn how to *react*, not how to *act* to satisfy themselves. Others are in neutral, ready to move ahead but needing something to get them going. With good intentions and an occasional sputter of enthusiasm, they wait.

Still others may decide not to get involved in a relationship at all. They fear losing control, being inadequate, making the wrong choice, or being rejected. They are counting their risks rather than their blessings. They need to redirect their energies toward life dreams they believe are attainable.

If you feel stuck and need to redirect your energies, you can do so by first examining your life dreams and then deciding to do something about them. By taking time to think about your dreams, you will find yourself getting unstuck. By organizing your thoughts, you will be able to decide what to do.

Exercise: **Is Something Holding You Back?**

Get comfortable and relax. Imagine being at your favorite place outdoors. Your favorite sounds and smells surround you. You hear the birds sing or the wind blow; you smell the trees or the freshly cut grass. As you let yourself relax, get in touch with what is really important for you in a loving relationship.

Then ask yourself, "Why am I not in a loving relationship now? What's holding me back?" Write down your answers.

_____

_____

_____

_____

_____

_____

_____

_____

_____

_____

Sometimes people feel frustrated and stuck just before they break out of their habitual ways of thinking. No one wants to volunteer for hard times, but it is often in the moments of darkness or strife that people ask themselves new questions and come up with new answers. Just as a seedling reaching for the sun starts from the darkness of the ground, dreams sometimes take form in frustration before they burst into light.

Going for Your Dreams!

Dreams seldom come true unless you are willing do something to make them come true. The dreaming is the easy part. Working to turn dreams into realities is more difficult and takes tenacity. It takes determination to get up every morning willing to face the day and move one step closer to your dream. It takes knowing that some dreams succeed and some fail. When they fail, it takes time to recuperate and gain a fresh viewpoint. You may have had a relationship or two that have not worked out. If so, you may need to say to yourself (and sometimes to others), "I will not give up. I will do what I have dreamed of doing, even if it takes more time and effort than I had expected." This is not an easy task, and it is one reason why some people choose to be alone or settle for less than they can get. You need to be decisive and persistent in your efforts to find the person who is right for you.

To prepare for that eventful meeting, you may need to take some private time to rekindle or expand on your dreams. People tend to think of new possibilities or create new dreams when they are relaxed, playing, or between one task and another so their minds are free to roam. At these moments, they are often more creative, see present and future realities from fresh perspectives, and find new solutions to old problems. They also find that dreaming of the future recharges their emotional batteries and leads to renewed hope and action. This can be true for you, if you decide to let go of some of your past and give yourself permission to create new dreams. Letting yourself dream of finding the right partner is the first step to making your dream come true.

Chapter 2

❧❧❧

MIND-SETS OF LOVE

"I don't believe in jumping in bed on the first date. And I'm not willing to change that attitude for anyone."

"My first husband was so critical, when we divorced I decided I'd never again be with a man like that. I'm looking for a man with an open mind who will respect my way of doing things."

"I remember deciding when I was a teenager that I was not going to get married until I was at least 28, so that I would marry the right person the first time around. I'm sure glad I gave myself some time to look around and not get too serious too quickly. It worked for me and I think that's what other people ought to do instead of getting married too young."

"Every time I get seriously involved with someone, something goes wrong. How can I figure out what I'm doing wrong so it won't happen the next time?"

"My boyfriend is convinced that once we get married, he doesn't want me to work. How can I change his mind without having to give him up?"

Most people make up their minds about how they *want* things to be or how things *should* be even before they meet a potential partner. When faced with circumstances that don't exactly fit their preconceived notions, some people insist on holding on tightly to their opinions, even if that makes it impossible for them to get what they want. Others decide that if their mind-sets are blocking them from getting what they want, they can do something to understand, modify, or change their minds and mind-sets.

Mind-sets are firmly held beliefs, opinions, and expectations. In psychological literature, mind-sets are often referred to as schemata, scripts, or frames of reference.[7] The word *mind-set* is used here instead because its meaning is more obvious and it is a more colloquially familiar term.

Mind-sets are built up through experience and provide order and predictability to life. Once formed, mind-sets are habits that spare people the task of having to make sense out of experience. That is, the person begins to rely on mind-sets rather than on reasoning about a situation itself. Consequently, mind-sets strongly influence how people perceive others and how they behave with others. People have mind-sets about all aspects of life, including love.

This chapter is about how mind-sets are formed and how your mind-sets may determine the entire course of your love life. You will discover ways to identify your mind-sets of love, as well as ways to modify those that might interfere with your finding the right partner.

Mind-Sets of Love

Mind-sets of love are important because people make up their minds about what they want and don't want even before they meet a potential partner. These mind-sets become the guiding principles or rules that affect how people act in the company of acquaintances, friends, and lovers.

Everyone has mind-sets of love. Sometimes these mind-sets are a help in finding the right partner; sometimes they are a hindrance. A helpful mind-set could be, "I'm interesting and most people like me when they get to know me." A hindering mind-set could be, "I don't have what it takes to make a long-term relationship work. I don't know how to open up to people."

A life dream, especially the dream of a right partner, is a particular kind of mind-set. Sometimes a life dream and a mind-set fit together, sometimes they don't. For example, a woman might have a *dream* of finding the right partner but a *mind-set* that contradicts her dream. She might believe that she is too old to fall in love again or that it is too much work to be involved in a relationship. The tension between a dream and a mind-set can account for much of the ambivalence or mood shifts that many people experience when in a relationship.

When mind-sets are positive and realistic, they make life easier. They guide a person's efforts in a successful direction. When they are inaccurate or negative, they can blind the person to other positive realities. Some people are not aware of the mind-sets that hinder them. They only know that things are not going the way they want them to. Other people are aware of the mind-sets that are interfering with their relationships but do not know how to change them. Negative mind-sets can be modified, replaced, or transcended. But first, people need to become aware of their own mind-sets and how they developed.

Earliest Mind-Sets of Love and Marriage

During childhood people make up their minds about who they are as individuals, how other people are, and how life operates. Children's mind-sets about love are first molded within the family, and especially by their parents. The parents serve as role models; their actions, advice, expectations, and even conflicts mold the child's mind-sets.[8]

Parents can be good models, bad models, or a bit of both—most parents provide the latter. If their marriage is happy and they enjoy each other and work well as a couple, it will serve as a good example of how to get along in a love relationship.

But if the parents are caught in conflict and power struggles, are distant and disinterested, are too busy to be involved, or are divorced, the children may repeat the same problematic patterns in later relationships. They may even avoid any kind of long-term relationships, believing that such relationships can't be successful. Or they may choose the opposite. They may decide never to get a divorce as their parents did and then stick to that decision, whether they are happy or miserable. Still others will commit themselves to work to make their relationship a success rather than a failure.

Observing what parents do is not the only way children's mind-sets are formed. All parents say many things. They give advice and directives to their children. Some are healthy and helpful, while some are not. A boy may benefit from being told "When you get married, make sure you pick a wife as energetic and loving as your mother." This gives the child a positive and productive mind-set. But some directives are considerably more rigid. A girl raised by a mother who continually warns her to "Never trust men" may never let herself get close to any man. This directive would be an obvious hindrance to her love life.

Parents have a major impact on the attitudes and behaviors of their children—but they can't take the credit or blame for everything. Children also develop mind-sets of their own during their school years.

The Impact of School Years

Besides being influenced by parents, children's mind-sets about love are also influenced by teachers, peers, books, and experiences they have in school. For example, a child who has many friends at school and learns to feel comfortable with kids of the opposite sex, has a good chance of becoming an adult who is likely to enjoy going to parties or other places where there are opportunities to meet potential dates. On the other hand, a child who was ignored or rejected by classmates may become an adult who doesn't want to risk further rejection and will act shy and withdrawn and avoid going to places where potential partners might be found.

In addition to mind-sets of love, children also develop mind-sets about their intelligence, social competence, and attractiveness in school years. These may be based on the comments of teachers or schoolmates. As adults, they may replay these comparisons to themselves when meeting or dating a potential partner. For example, a boy teased in school for not speaking English as well as the other students may, as an adult, experience a paralyzed feeling when meeting someone new. His mind may go blank or he may feel tongue-tied or stumble over his words. Or a girl who at an early age develops large breasts may feel embarrassed and wear loose blouses and hunch her shoulders to hide them. She may develop the mind-set that her body is ugly and, when grown up, may not allow herself to enjoy having her body touched in a sexually intimate relationship.

Experiences such as moving midyear from one school to another can also have a long-lasting effect on a child's self-image. Children with many friends in one community usually feel uprooted by a move and often have difficulty making friends in a new school and feel as if they don't belong. Feeling different may become a mind-set that remains with them even into college and adult years, haunting them whenever they are in new groups of people. On the other hand, children who move to a new community may meet a new group of peers with whom they immediately feel comfortable. This social success usually leads to increased sense of self-confidence which can also remain with them the rest of their lives.

For example, when Kim was a child her family moved at least once every year. As a result, she felt lonely and believed she would never have close friends or be part of the in crowd. Finally when she was 11 years old, her family decided to settle in a community they liked. For the first time in her life, Kim was able to put down roots in a school and make lasting friends. These relationships helped her modify her mind-set. Now at 21 she believes, "I don't have to feel lonely; I can make real and lasting friendships with people who care about me."

Luckily for most children, the early school years are a mixture of experiences, both easy and difficult, pleasurable and agonizing. Mind-sets developed in school may be reconfirmed or modified in adolescent and teenage years.

Early Dating and Teenage Love

By the time a child becomes a teenager, he or she has already formed many preliminary mind-sets about love and relationships. Yet there are many new experiences that teenagers go through that can leave lasting impressions on their mind-sets. Factors such as popularity, dating, appearance, socioeconomic or ethnic background, intelligence, health, and the experience of first love make the teenage years a challenge. The challenge may dislodge old mind-sets and serve as motivation to form new ones.

Many teenagers take life and love quite seriously. When they begin dating, they are exposed to new opportunities and choices. They learn about how to act in different social situations and they try out their emerging identity as adults. Some kids date frequently, others seldom. But most make important decisions about their attractiveness and self-worth based on these experiences.

Eileen was an A student, but she noticed that most boys were not interested in dating smart girls. They seemed to want girls that were more interested in being sociable or sexy. She soon felt that being popular was more important than good grades so she began to act dumb in class and joke around with the boys. As she got more and more dates her grades dropped lower and lower. Eventually she realized that by acting dumb she was attracting boys—but not necessarily the ones she liked. She decided to stop hiding her intellectual abilities and to look for a boyfriend who would like her for who she was.

As adolescents go through puberty and their bodies and emotions go through rapid changes, they often make important decisions about themselves. In high school, Joel was teased about having acne. He developed a mind-set that women would not want to kiss him because his face was scarred and unattractive, and even after his skin problems subsided, this stopped him from getting close to women later on.

Teenagers have a great deal of curiosity about the opposite sex and many are anxious to experience what it feels like to fall in love for the first time. The first "true love" often leaves lasting impressions and some people remember a high school sweetheart for the rest of their lives.

When first love goes well, people discover that being in love is one of the true pleasures in life. If a person's first love experience doesn't go well or ends in disappointment, he or she may shrug it off and look for a better relationship or feel hesitant about future dating. Even a positive experience may be interpreted differently by different people.

For example, a teenager who goes steady for a long time with the same person in high school learns early how to deal with the ups and downs of a relationship and often develops a mind-set that a close relationship is possible and worthwhile. In contrast, others who go steady for several years might feel they have missed out on a lot of opportunities and develop a mind-set that it doesn't pay to get serious.

One of the important choices teenagers make is whether or not to be sexually active and, if so, with whom. If their early sexual experimentation is gradual and feels safe and loving, they will look forward to adult sexual relationships. A girl who learns how to be assertive and to set comfortable limits will likely trust herself and future dates. A boy who understands how to act responsibly will likely feel the same.

On the other hand, if early sexual experiences go awry and perhaps a pregnancy results, or if a teenager gets a bad reputation because of an unfortunate romance that becomes the talk of the school, those involved may remember the pain and unhappiness for years and hesitate to get close to someone in the future. More seriously, a teenager who is molested or raped may be haunted by the trauma for years. Later she or he may avoid or end a potentially "right" relationship because of the mind-set due to the experience and avoid dealing with the frustration, discomfort, or disgust experienced in the past. Without reviewing the innumerable kinds of experiences teenagers go through, it is obvious that these years are pivotal in the formation of mind-sets of love.

Exercise: Early Messages You Were Given

Think about the important messages you got when you were little and the decisions you made about whether those messages were right or wrong. Next, fill in the following incomplete sentences to help yourself identify those messages.

Men are _____
Husbands should _____
Women are _____
Wives should _____
Marriage is _____
People in love should _____

Which of these messages did you believe and incorporate into your mind-set? How have these messages affected you? Are they a help or a hindrance? How might you rewrite these sentences today?

Men are _____

Husbands should _____

Women are _____

Wives should _____

Marriage is _____

People in love should _____

Exercise: Young Love Experiences

Think about your parents' impact on your life. Did you ever pick a partner who was very similar to one of your parents? If so, what did you learn from that relationship?

_____
_____
_____
_____
_____
_____
_____
_____
_____
_____
_____

Think back to your first love. What memories and feelings do you still have about it? Did that relationship have any long-lasting effect on you?

_____

_____

_____

_____

_____

_____

_____

_____

_____

_____

The Effects of Past Partners on New Relationships

Attitudes about love and life are not necessarily fixed at age 7, 14, or 21. Mind-sets can be modified by significant adult relationships. Experiences in adult love relationships may reconfirm previously held mind-sets or may create new ones. These new mind-sets can be positive and valuable or negative and frustrating.

People frequently carry with them the habits or ghosts of previous relationships, either consciously or unconsciously; these patterns may be dreaded or desired. They may expect to fight or have sex with their new partner the way they did with their last one. They may also expect to handle finances, celebrate holidays, and get along with their in-laws as they did in their previous relationship.

Sometimes when people move from one relationship to another, they become more aware of what they want in the right partner. The lessons learned in one relationship are often taken to the next, and they can be of great value. For example, Sharon believed in healthy nutrition. She read and talked about it and prepared well-balanced meals. For Dennis nutrition had little importance. He was used to eating hot dogs, French fries, and TV dinners. After living with Sharon for several years, he came to understand the importance of nutrition. He even grew to prefer healthier meals. He changed both his diet and his mind-set about eating. In this way, her mind-set became his. His new mind-set stayed with him even after their marriage ended. When he began dating again, he paid close attention to what his partners ate and sometimes even gave them a lecture on the importance of well-balanced meals.

Relationships that are painful also influence people's mind-sets. A man who finds out his wife is having an affair may form a new mind-set: "I'll never trust or love anyone again." This can be an understandable reaction at the moment, but it is too restrictive a decision to live for the rest of one's life. This man needs to modify or eventually change his mind-set. Otherwise when dating other women he will tend to be distrustful and imagine they will also be unfaithful.

Jessica modified her mind-set of how a wife "should" be after she had been married for many years to George, a corporate vice president. She explained with great emotion, "I felt like I was a piece of the expensive and beautiful furniture. He gave his cars more attention than he gave me. In front of other people, he made me feel as if I should keep my mouth shut and pretend that everything between us was perfect when it wasn't. When I tried to talk to friends about how selfish he was and how lonely I felt, they would say things like 'Nonsense, he's a wonderful man. He loves you, and besides, you have everything any woman would ever want.' Then one day I got so fed up with the charade that I left, without really knowing what had gone wrong. It was only after two years of separation that I could understand. Since then I've decided that I will never again let anyone treat me like that!" Decisions such as Jessica's—to change habitual ways of thinking, feeling, and behaving—usually require a great deal of motivation and courage.

Consciously evaluating previous relationships is often a useful way for people to discover what they want and don't want in a relationship. If their previous relationships were good, they may want to duplicate or approximate some of those enjoyable aspects in future partnerships. Even when a relationship doesn't work out, it is important to ask "What positive lesson did I learn from this relationship that will make my next one far better?" If a previous relationship was disappointing, you can use it as a clue to identify the mind-sets you live by so you can change the ones that hinder you. It is easy to walk away from a past relationship with unhappy memories and self-protective mind-sets, but they don't lead to better love. Learning positive lessons from the past will make a successful future more probable.

Exercise: An Interview by Past Loves

When people remember their past relationships, they may not recognize the evolution of their attitudes toward love. This brief exercise can highlight the evolution your mind-sets have gone through.

Take a few minutes and make a list of your ex-loves. Put them in chronological order beginning from early childhood. Make a few notes on how each one was right for you in some way and how each one was wrong for you.

Now imagine each one of them is with you now and interviewing you. Each will ask you the same question, "What did you learn from our relationship?" Answer the questions spontaneously and on the list you made, record each answer.

Look for patterns in the kinds of partners you have chosen.
Then notice how your mind-sets grew, changed, and evolved.

Who:

_____

_____

How he/she was right for me:

_____

_____

How he/she was wrong for me:

_____

_____

What I learned from the relationship:

_____

_____

Other Forces That Influence Your Mind-Sets

There are other factors that precondition people's thinking
about themselves and their choice of partners. These forces
include their cultural norms, their expectations of the roles of men
and women, their religious background, and their socioeconomic
needs and realities. Each can exert a strong influence on your
mind-sets of love.

Cultural mind-sets develop as people incorporate the logic and
wisdom, as well as the prejudice and parochialism, of the cultures
in which they grow up. Most people more or less conform to their
culture in order to be validated as one of the group and to prove
they fit in. Many people take their cultural mind-sets for granted

and expect that everyone else should live as they do. This can lead to problems.

Each culture or subculture has different values and expectations. How and when a person should date and get married varies from one culture to another. For example, in Ireland it is common for men to first marry in their late 30s; in South America men often get married in their teen years or early 20s. In some countries, people choose their partners freely; in other countries, dating and marriage is managed by the parents, and class compatibility is frequently considered a crucial factor in choosing a partner.[9]

Some cultures have mind-sets that do not accept dating or marrying someone outside one's group; other cultures freely accept, even welcome, people from different backgrounds. People who date or marry cross-culturally are often seeking to balance the characteristics of their own ethnic background with those of their partner's. They may be moving away from some values of their culture as they move toward different values in the other culture. Their differences in culture can be a refreshing change from the sameness of their own kind. Yet family and friends may be critical and consider their choice unwise, disloyal, or doomed to eventual failure. This is often a hard current to go against.

Culture shock can occur when one person takes the mind-set of one culture into another one. This is a challenge that faces those who date and marry someone of a different nationality or who move to another country. But culture shock is experienced not only by those who move from one nation to another. For example, if someone raised on the East Coast—where she has close lifelong ties to family and neighborhood friends—moves to the West Coast—where people are often easier to meet but harder to get to know—the friendships and closeness so commonly experienced as part of the East Coast life can be sorely missed. In situations like this, the person may expect her partner to fill all the social needs that were filled by many different people back home.

People from one subculture often feel like a duck out of water in another subculture. Claudia was raised in a small Midwest farming community. As an adult, she moved to Chicago and started her search for a partner who was still interested in a good old-fashioned woman—which she defined as a housewife and mother involved in school and the community. But in the urban culture, she didn't know where to look for someone with values similar to hers. It took her several frustrating years to get to know where to meet her kind of people.

Each culture has unique expectations for men and women while dating, when in love, and when married. In the United States mind-sets of what men and women are like and how they should or should not act are rapidly changing.[10] Previously, a common mind-set was that a woman's place is in the home. Now more people believe that a woman's place is in the office as well. Previously, men were not believed to be capable of raising their children after divorce. Now many men are choosing to retain custody of their children and raise them quite well.

Other cultures have very different expectations. Some have serious legal ramifications. For example, in some Latin American countries a legal double standard remains very strong. A man can easily obtain a divorce but women must prove "extreme cruelty." Even if granted a divorce, women seldom receive child or spousal support or a fair property settlement. Consequently, many married women have a secret "bail-out" savings account in case their relationship ends in divorce. When picking a partner, financial security is a crucial factor to their final choice.

Everyone interprets experience through the filters of their preconceived mind-sets. Furthermore, research has shown that people look for evidence to confirm their mind-sets and tend to only remember events that agree with them. People also tend to be selective and tune out, discount, or reject information that is inconsistent, contradictory, or does not fit what they believe to be true. In addition, most people have stereotypes of other groups and often notice only those people that fit their stereotype expectations.[11] In other words, people tend to see only what they already believe is true. These mind-sets lead people to misinterpret each other.

Even in the same culture there are differences on how people interpret the same event. For example, some men believe it is appropriate to open the door of the car for their date, to seat her in a restaurant, and to pay the bill inconspicuously. Some women might feel thrilled by this or at least agree that this is the way a date ought to behave. Other women might feel offended by these attentions, believing that such behavior is condescending and chauvinistic or that the hidden agenda behind such courtesy is sex. If a woman believes all men are fickle and her boyfriend takes female business associates out to dinner, she may jump to the conclusion that he's being unfaithful to her. Inaccurate or irrational cultural mind-sets can interfere with the search for happiness and prevent people from finding their right partner.

Religious mind-sets develop because religious experiences and traditions influence many mind-sets, especially those of love, sex, and marriage. These religious mind-sets may be so deeply rooted that they are not brought into question until challenged during dating or marriage, especially in an interfaith or "mixed" relationship. For example, if a woman involved in a conservative religious group dates a man who does not believe in religion, she will doubt he is right for her. He, too, may doubt and wonder if her religious convictions will become a barrier to their relationship.

For some religious people, interfaith partnerships do not work easily. For others, dating people with a different religious background is comfortable and not a big issue. However, these same people sometimes find that their parents, friends or clergy have mind-sets against their dating or getting married. Will his Jewish parents accept his Catholic girlfriend? Will her priest encourage or discourage their relationship?

Religious conflicts that are easy to avoid while dating may become a major dilemma when wedding plans are made. Each person may feel caught in a bind. They may start arguing when thinking about the kind of ceremony they want, who will perform it, where it will be held, etc. Some couples decide that their religious differences are too much to ignore and call it quits. Others decide that their religious backgrounds are not important in their decision. Still others decide that their religious differences are not enough reason to avoid a relationship when they have found a partner who is right in so many other ways.

Economic mind-sets can also influence the selection of a partner. Some people have a mind-set that money and position are everything, that "you can't get anywhere unless you make big bucks." For them money is a measure of success. For other people, money means security—the security of buying a house, saving for old age, etc.

Money is often a touchy subject and many people feel uncomfortable talking about it. Some couples may avoid the subject when dating, only to find out later how important it is for their future.

Some people enjoy being organized and handling their finances carefully. They keep their checkbooks balanced and pay their bills and taxes on time. Others dread this as a nuisance, and consider bookkeeping as theoretically a good idea but personally inconsequential and a waste of time. They don't like being bothered and prefer to have others do it for them. Still others play money games by spending more than they earn and not keeping track of it until eventually they find themselves in financial trouble.

It is important to know your mind-sets about money so that when dating you can talk freely about what it means to you and find out what it means to your partner. Otherwise you may find yourself feeling disappointed like Erica. Erica expected Howard to treat her as her father had treated her mother. Daddy had given Erica's mother his paycheck and let her make all the financial decisions and spend their money as she wanted. But Howard was not willing to live like that. He wanted to handle things as *his* father had. Howard's father was very strong and controlling. He demanded that things be done his way and made all the decisions about how and when to spend money. This was a big disappointment for Erica. She was used to a certain lifestyle, and expected the same or better in her love relationship. When it didn't happen, money became a focal point of frequent arguments between them.

Some people feel intimidated by the economic success and prestige of a partner and let that interfere with an otherwise good relationship. For example, Danny was a carpenter in his late 20s when he met Margaret. She was a junior executive in a highly successful business. Their first encounters were passionate and intense. The relationship was going along well until she invited him to a party at the home of one of her associates. When they went, Danny started acting nervous and agitated. He told her that he was "only a carpenter" and that her friends were "corporate hot shots." He felt embarrassed to drive up to her associate's large suburban house in his pickup truck. He said he wouldn't know how to act or what he might have in common to talk about with her friends. Shortly after this, Danny pulled back from the relationship. His mind-sets about himself and his socioeconomic realities were more powerful than his affection for her.

Updating Your Mind-Sets

Do you want to stay the way you are, or are there any mind-sets you want or need to change? People who do not examine their mind-sets carefully may go off in search of a relationship with preconceived notions that over and over again interfere with their happiness. Or they may get started in a relationship and then do something to sabotage it, like acting too casual, too cautious, too helpless, too aggressive, too demanding, or too possessive. They may start to get close but then hesitate, unable to go the next step, but unsure as to why they are unable to make a deeper commitment.

Exercise: **Mind-Sets and Choices**

Think about the mind-sets you've incorporated from the people in cultures around you. These may play an important part in your perception or preference of who is right for you.

List a cultural mind-set you have.

_____

_____

How does this mind-set influence your choice of a partner?

_____

_____

List a religious mind-set you have.

_____

_____

How does this mind-set influence your choice of a partner?

_____

_____

List a socio-economic mind-set you have.

_____

_____

How does this mind-set influence your choice of a partner?

_____

_____

_____

_____

Any person limited by restrictive mind-sets needs to find the courage and inner power to break free of them. Breaking free of old mind-sets feels like being freed of a heavy burden. Instead of seeing the world with blinders, people then open themselves to new possibilities and new perspectives.

Mind-sets are resistant to change and to update them takes some thoughtful effort. But with the right motivation, a clear strategy, and enough effort, almost *any* mind-set can be changed! If you have a mind-set that you want to change, here is a strategy that works.

Exercise: How to Change a Mind-Set

Relax and get comfortable. Think about the mind-sets you live by and especially those that have emotional impact on you. Assess which ones are working for you and which are getting in the way of finding your right partner. Next, ask yourself:

What mind-set do I want to change?

_____

_____

What new mind-set do I want to live by instead?

_____

_____

What am I willing to do to change my mind-set?

_____

_____

_____

What could I say to myself to reinforce my new mind-set?

_____

_____

_____

How will I act differently when I've completed this change?

_____

_____

_____

Find ways to nurture and reinforce your new mind-set. One way is to keep your dreams of love in mind and to think positively about getting what you want. Keep in mind your reasons for wanting to change your inhibiting mind-set. Some people create new phrases or affirmations to tell themselves. For example: "I know I'm worth it!" or "I know that if I really want something, I can usually make it happen." These kinds of self-supporting thoughts can make a great difference.

Others visualize living their new mind-set. To do this, create a collage that expresses how you want to be. Hung on your wall, it becomes a positive reminder. Research shows that people who visualize themselves succeeding have a better chance of success.[12]

Still others find examples of other people (either living or fictional) who live by their newly chosen mind-set. Keeping these models in mind makes it easier to imagine how to act in the future.

Some people find it hard to know which mind-sets to change; others know which ones they want to change, but find it hard to make the change. Some people are able to do it by themselves; others need help. Some mind-sets are so painful or so entrenched that is useful to consider working with a psychotherapist or counselor.

Updating a mind-set is a learning experience that allows people to recognize the whys and hows of their thoughts, feelings, and actions. As you learn to understand yourself better, you'll learn to understand relatives, friends, and lovers in more realistic and compassionate ways. This understanding increases your chances of finding and creating a successful and long-lasting relationship.

Remember to give yourself credit for the mind-sets you've already changed in your life and remind yourself that you can do it again! Give yourself time to learn how to live by your new mind-set. It takes time to establish new habits, especially mind-sets that you will use to direct your life in the future. Be patient, don't expect overnight changes. And remember, once you are sure that your new mind-set will work, you'll truly be able to let go of the old one.

Chapter 3

∽οχοχο∾

MEETING THE ONE
YOU'VE BEEN WAITING FOR

"It was raining. I was sitting by the fire thinking about some past dates that were fun and exciting. Then I got uptight. Since I've moved to this city, I don't know where to go to meet people. It's not as easy as you might think to find someone special."

"My mother always told me to be careful of men because they were only interested in sex. I don't think that's true. The men I've been meeting only like to talk about their jobs!"

"I get all dressed up and ready to go out to try to meet someone; then I panic and get a stomachache and stay home."

"I've being thinking it would be nice to join a health club. I'm not an exercise fanatic but I do like to look good. Maybe I'll even meet someone interesting there, who knows? Or maybe I should try something different like a weekend at a ski resort. There're always interesting people skiing. But what if I go and no one notices me? What if all the good catches are taken and I get stuck with a loser? I don't want to make a fool of myself, yet I have to start somewhere."

Some people have no problem meeting others. They're naturals at it because they are interested in getting to know new people, even if it means risking an encounter that may fizzle out. They believe that getting stuck by an occasional thorn is better than having no roses at all. Such people often attract friends and lovers with a similar sense of self-esteem and sociability. Because they are friendly and relaxed, they have no shortage of dates.

On the other hand, there are those who are constantly critical about little or big issues. They have a harder time meeting potential partners because they expect to be disappointed. When they do meet someone, their judgments are made quickly and harshly. They also have such high standards for themselves that they hold themselves back from getting acquainted for fear of being criticized or judged inadequate.

This chapter explains how dreams and mind-sets influence each other and how the mind-sets you have can help you or hinder you from meeting the person of your dreams. It will also show you how people use "time" as an explanation for their success or frustration in going for their dreams. This chapter also deals with the importance of first impressions, how to evaluate your impressions of the other person and how to present yourself to make the right impression. You will learn about the subtle messages you may be sending and what to do if you keep people away or if you are attracting the wrong partners. The last section of this chapter will give you important hints on how and where to meet the one you have been waiting for.

Dreams Versus Mind-Sets

Everyone has dreams of love in the future and they have mind-sets that may help or hinder them from achieving their dreams. When people have conflicts between their dreams and their mind-sets, they usually hold themselves back from meeting people and falling in love. The conflicts feel like an internal war that has no end and only temporary reprises. One minute a person will feel enthusiastic about relationships, the next minute discouraged. Back and forth they Ping-Pong through their internal conflict until one or the other side wins. To counterbalance the ambivalent feelings between the mind-set and the dream, they create an explanation that justifies their dilemma. This naturally affects the way they feel and act about potential meetings. The following are a sampling of mind-sets about being single, and how these mind-sets can prevent people from finding the love of their life.

Dream: I want to be happy whether I'm single or married.

Mind-Set: But I can't really be happy unless I'm married.

Some people don't feel good about themselves if they are not paired up with someone. These people imagine that if they were married it would prove they are lovable and part of the mainstream of life. This has been called the the "Noah's Ark factor," by psychologist Penelope Russianoff. It is "the perception that the whole world is populated by couples and that you, too, have to be part of a couple in order to belong."[13]

Most single people say they would like to get married. But they also ask themselves, "At what cost?" For many, the possibility of jeopardizing their careers, changing the way they live, or going through the ups and downs of a relationship is simply not worth it. They have to come to terms with staying single rather than settling for Mr. or Ms. Wrong.

There are many reasons people remain single. We tend to categorize single people depending on our own mind-set. If you met a man in his 40s, who is good looking, professionally successful, and has never been married, what would your first impression of him be? Some people would think, "What's wrong with him? Why isn't he married? Isn't he interested in women?" Some might wonder if he's shy, or overly attached to his mother, or terribly lonely, or hostile toward women, or gay. Still others might imagine that he lives a wild life with a new affair each week.

If you met a woman under the same conditions, would you have the same reactions? Would you jump to the same conclusions or would you think something different? Technically the word *spinster* refers to a woman who has never been married, just as *bachelor* refers to a man who has never been married. But spinster often carries with it a social stigma; the connotation that a woman couldn't "get" a man because of bad luck, bad looks, or bad personality. Bachelor usually doesn't carry the same stigma. A man is often given credit for having chosen to remain single; the woman is discredited for not being chosen. This archaic attitude of respecting a man's decision to not marry and attributing a woman's single status to supposed inadequacies is still common and often reinforced by the fantasy that single men are better able to take care of themselves emotionally and financially than women. This mind-set leads to a great deal of discouragement and misunderstanding.

Debbie had an aunt who never married. At a family gathering Debbie remarked, "Poor Auntie Jean—the train left her behind. I'm glad she has us, otherwise she wouldn't have anyone to take care of her." One of Debbie's cousins answered, "No, Aunt Jean wasn't left behind. She used to have a secret lover and when he left her, she never recovered from the blow." A second cousin chimed in, "The real reason she's alone is that she is still tied to her father who has a harsh personality." "No," a third interrupted, "I just think she knows the importance of being choosey." Nobody in the family knew the truth about Aunt Jean's single status. Each person had a different interpretation, based on their particular mind-set.

Someone not locked into this Noah's Ark mind-set might think, "Who wants to be stuck in a relationship with someone that in time I might feel trapped by?" A bachelor at 43, Roger explained, "I'm single and I'm happy the way I am. I don't have any intention of getting married. It's not that I don't like women, I just like being able to live the way I do and not having to answer to anybody or take care of anybody. When I meet people for the first time and they learn that I've never been married, they usually seem shocked. When I was younger, they used to ask me when was I going to get married. Now they just stare at me and imagine I'm weird or something."

Being single, you may feel uncomfortable and distrustful when meeting someone new, or you may feel OK with your single status yet still feel a brief shiver of discomfort from time to time. If you find yourself feeling uncomfortable, accept it as a feeling of situational dissatisfaction. Check yourself out to see if you are sure you want a relationship or if you have too much internal resistance to getting attached. If you experience a great deal of ambivalence in this way, it may be useful to seek counseling to sort out your dreams from your mind-sets and to get on with your efforts toward success.

Dream: I want the best!

Mind-Set: But all the good catches are already taken.

When it comes to picking a partner, few people imagine themselves as choosing anything but the best. The problem is that sometimes it can seem like all the good catches are taken. Research conducted by Neil Bennett, Patricia Craig, and David Bloom painted a bleak picture for women.[14] They concluded that the older a college-educated woman gets, the less are her chances of getting married. With age, it becomes harder for her to find a compatible partner. Therefore, she may become hopeless and avoid meetings that could open the door to new relationships. But studies like this only present statistical averages, not personal odds. Your possibilities and probabilities depend on your unique attitude and approach.

Some single people are not "good catches." They are hard to please and harder to live with. Living alone often makes people more set in their ways and less willing to compromise. They may become so particular that it would be nearly impossible for anyone to live up to their expectations.

Of course, everyone, whether single or married, has some part of their personality which is hard to live with—even for themselves! It is the part of the personality they prefer to hide and not have others know about. Composed of fears, anger, fantasies, and secrets, this dark side of the personality has been referred to as "the shadow."[15] If you look hard enough and close enough at anyone, you can spot their shadow. Yet if you see only the shadow in a person, you will be turned off and stop a potentially good relationship before it ever has a chance to emerge. If you are realistic and curious, you will find out about all sides of the person and find out if the pluses outweigh the minuses.

Above all, keep in mind there *are* many good potentials out there. Some haven't been married or have been widowed and may be finally ready to consider a long-term relationship. Others have been divorced, but that doesn't mean they are neurotic or hard to live with. If you really believe all the good catches are taken, this implies that you're not a good catch either, and you know that's not true. You are right for somebody, maybe several somebodies. But in order to find them, you first must let go of the mind-set that all the good catches are taken.

Dream: I want to get married and settle down.

Mind-Set: But I only meet men/women who just want to have fun.

Some people imagine singles are always living it up and going to exciting places every weekend—as if Club Med was their home base. People who say that singles "only want to have fun" usually mean that singles are not very mature or responsible or are not interested in making a commitment to a long-term relationship. Their mind-set is "Even if I do date someone, it will be a waste of my time, energy, and effort. In the end, I'll be disappointed and empty-handed. How can I be happy with someone who doesn't take life seriously? I want someone who will be committed to our relationship and will work hard to make good things happen and I can't seem to find someone like that."

This mind-set is a hindrance because it is more myth than truth. Single people are not always on the go, living a life of excitement and adventure. Like everyone else, often they are too tired to go out. They may be home reading a book, working in the yard, or trying to cook and take care of kids after a full day's work. In between all this, they may be trying to find time to shop, pay bills, or just collapse in front of the television.

If you have this mind-set, you already expect the relationship to be shallow and go nowhere. Therefore, it can stop you from meeting potential partners even before you get to know them. The truth is, people often fall in love when they share moments of fun. Having fun is one of the things that brings couples closer. In addition, it could be worthwhile to find out about a person's fun side as well as other aspects of his or her personality. Does this person have depth? Can he or she be serious as well as fun?

People who can laugh together can often think together or even cry together. If you do meet someone who seems to have an excessive need to have fun, remember that that person might just be trying to heal a deep wound from the past. Try talking about what's important to you and ask the other person about what's important to them. You might find that beneath the surface, there is a person with an honest desire to find someone who really cares, someone like yourself. You may even find that person wants to get married and settle down once the right person is found.

Dream: I want a good sex life.

Mind-Set: But most single people are *only* interested in sex or they're *not* interested in sex at all!

Some people believe that most singles are sex starved and always on the prowl. Some seem to be! They treat sex as a recreational activity or a conquest-and-conquer event and discount their partners' emotions and dreams.

Others, out of a need for reassurance, go through a period of promiscuity after getting divorced or breaking up with someone they loved. They feel unattractive and fear no one will ever be interested in them, so they try to prove that they are still attractive. This was the case for Loretta, a 42-year-old divorced woman who had been married for twenty years and hadn't had sex for the last five years of her marriage. Her husband was always "too tired" and "not in the mood." Every night for the first six months following her divorce, she went to a singles' bar and picked someone up. At first it was exciting to be treated as an attractive sexual being once again. Eventually, though, the excitement wore off and she discovered that she really wanted a meaningful and long-lasting relationship, not only sex.

Some people respond quite differently after divorce. They become celibate. For instance, after a hard and stormy second marriage, Marilyn felt so disappointed in men that she decided to make herself scarce and unavailable. She refused all dates and organized her life around her kids, her work, and her friends. She didn't want to meet anyone new so she didn't.

People who have either mind-set—that all people want is sex or that the right people aren't interested in sex at all—may wonder, "How will I ever meet someone who is sexually compatible for me? There are no safe places to go. I can't joke around and have fun without other people thinking that I'm making a pass at them. I want to be close and intimate with the right person, but I don't want to be considered 'easy or available' and turn the relationship into a sexual frenzy." The opposite type of person, someone who is frightened or angry at being expected to be sexual or expected to perform, often *avoids* relationships. If you have either of these mind-sets, you may stop yourself from going places so that you can avoid the sexual pressures, expectations, or letdowns. This type of lifestyle won't help you find a compatible partner.

In reality, many people want a good sexual relationship but do not make it their top priority. Security, companionship, honest communication, and other qualities are much more important to them.

To increase your possibilities of finding the right partner, set some sexual guidelines for yourself. If you think about what is right for you before you get in an uncomfortable situation, your decisions will be easier to make and maintain.

Dream: I want my friends to accept me as I am.

Mind-Set: But couples don't want single people around.

Have you ever heard someone say that couples don't want their single friends around because they are "rivals" or a temptation to their spouse? Couples who feel this way seldom trust each other. They feel insecure and suffer from jealousy or they already have a relationship that is on the rocks.

For Karen, it was painful to realize that her married women friends started to keep her at distance after her divorce because they thought she would flirt with their husbands. "My friends were not the same after my divorce. They didn't see me as a friend anymore. They saw me as their enemy, as a threat, as someone they had to be careful with. I'm not interested in their husbands. I just want to be friends like we used to be." Karen was trying to adapt to a world she was no longer part of. She felt confused and let down by her friends who did not stand by her in her transition. It was hard for her to accept their rejection. She began to feel very insecure in other meetings.

Some singles feel uncomfortable becoming good friends with another person's spouse, because they are concerned that their intentions might be misinterpreted. If you feel like this, you need to decide which married friends you want to keep and which ones you don't. The couples to keep as friends are those who will welcome you in their home, be supportive, and be willing to share their family and friends with you. They may even become a resource for introducing you to other eligible single people. Some people enjoy being matchmakers for their friends.

Another aspect of this mind-set is being uncomfortable as the only single among a group of couples, feeling like a "fifth wheel." To avoid being held back by this mind-set, some people have friends they ask to fill in as a date when "couples only" kinds of situations arise. Others find that meeting a couple is easier in many ways than meeting a single because it is easier to start a conversation by getting them to talk about their first date, their marriage, their kids, and so on. If you have a mind-set about being a single person among couples, you might raise the topic with your friends to check out your perception. Perhaps they don't mind having single friends and you've misinterpreted the situation.

Exercise: Making Your Mind-Sets Work for You

Not everyone has conflict between their dreams and mind-sets. This exercise is for those who do. Fill in the blanks to reflect your dilemma and also how you could change it if you chose to.

One of my dreams: _____

_____

A mind-set that interferes with my dream: _____

_____

The effect these conflicting attitudes has on my meeting people:

_____

_____

How I might change my thinking and my mind-set to be more

supportive of my dream:

_____

_____

When Will the Time Come?

People tend to be defensive when things go wrong or if they expect things to go wrong. Defenses are unconscious protective mechanisms against being hurt, rejected, or left empty-handed again. They are often expressed as internal or external statements of justification.

People get defensive when they have a dream of who and what they want, yet also have a mind-set that counteracts their dream. Although they want to go for their dream, their mind-set holds them back, often creating ambivalent feelings about what to do.

To deal with this ambivalence, they often create a defensive explanation that justifies their dilemma. These explanations are often referred to as "time problems."[16] Time excuses postpone the time for taking action to meet that someone special.

A common time defense is: "I won't meet a compatible partner *until* I have lost twenty pounds or *until* the children are grown and gone or *until* I finish my degree." Other common time explanations or excuses are:

- "I would like to date but I *never* really have time to."

- "I don't want to go because I *always* meet the wrong person."

- "It doesn't matter anyway—*after* we get close, something is bound to go wrong."

- "I don't want to get serious *until* I'm financially stable."

- "I *always* say the wrong thing."

- "I *almost* fell in love but then I found out he/she was married."

People who defend themselves using time excuses are often waiting for something magical to happen. They are protecting themselves from the fear of failure by thinking in terms of time: never, almost, until, always, after, and so on. The time explanations people create are often used regardless of what the conflicting dreams and mind-set might be. Ambivalence about choosing an option and taking action holds them back.

Exercise: **What's Your Time Explanation?**

To discover the time explanations you give yourself, complete the following statements as they apply to meeting people:

"I never _____

_____

"I almost _____

_____

"I always _____

_____

"Until I _____

_____

"After I _____

_____

Once you've identified your time explanation, it is easier to recognize how you stop yourself from getting involved in a relationship that can work. With this awareness, you can begin to think of a new time mind-set that is more positive and hopeful. Free of inhibiting mind-sets and time excuses, you can get out there and meet someone new.

First Impressions

Meeting people doesn't have to be hard. All of us meet vast numbers of people in our lifetime. Yet, for better or worse, first impressions often determine whether or not people meet, to whom they are attracted, and what they chose to do after they meet. There have been some studies about first impressions that confirm what many consider common knowledge:

- First impressions are influenced by information known about the person before the first encounter.

- People give greater importance to negative information about someone than positive information.

- People's names have impact on how others first perceive them.

- Meeting someone in a positive environment increases that person's attractiveness.

- People's general tendency or predisposition to evaluate others favorably or negatively influences their overall impressions of someone they first meet.

- When people feel good, they tend to like people more when they first meet them.[17]

First impressions can determine whether a relationship gets started or not. Have you ever looked at someone across a crowded room and known that he or she was someone you wanted to get to know? Positive first impressions can be a powerful motivation for approaching someone new. It can be the sparkle in her eyes, the way he walks, the way she moves, or the way he talks that catches your interest. This is how it was for Jesse; "When I saw Meryl across the crowded dance floor, I started walking toward her. I knew she was the one. I wasn't surprised when she started walking toward me. It was as if our actions were synchronized and rehearsed beforehand. When we met, I just looked at her and said 'I love the way you dance.' Then I actually kissed her on the side of the cheek and introduced myself. I've never acted that way before, but I was so enchanted by her. It was as if we were out of time and space." Meryl also remembers that moment. She knew the first moment she saw Jesse that he would be special in her life. Their first meeting was so strong it felt almost spiritual, something that could not be put into words.

For many people, the first impression is not so earthshaking. Wedding bells don't ring and fireworks don't go off. Yet there is a significant sense of a shared attitude toward life that, developed over time, becomes a strong bond.

Exercise: What Catches Your Interest?

Close your eyes for a moment and imagine you are being introduced to someone. What do you notice first? Do you pay close attention to factors such as race, age, clothing, height, body structure, facial features, color of hair? Do you pay more attention to looks or to personality? Are you attracted to someone who is gregarious, quiet, independent, or needy?

What Attracts Me	*What I Don't Care About*
_____	_____
_____	_____
_____	_____
_____	_____
_____	_____

Beauty Is in the Eye of the Beholder

Appearance and attractiveness have a strong effect on first impressions and consequently on how people respond to each other. Beliefs about attractiveness are influenced by the times and place in which people live. For example, in some eras and some locales, voluptuous women have been considered attractive. In contemporary Western society, however, women strive to be thin.

Almost everyone wants to look their best. This is why millions and millions of dollars are spent each year in ads to convince people to invest their money on cosmetics, clothes, and health products. Women, in particular, face strong societal pressure, reinforced by movies, television, and advertising, to alter their physical appearance to fit the current trends.

The reality is, however, that people come in all shapes and sizes and, more often than not, don't fit the mode that's "in." Depending on current styles, most people want to adapt to them so they will be considered attractive. If being tall is desirable, women may buy ultra-high heels. Padded bras, popular in the 1950s, may help if "buxom" is stylish; breast reduction through plastic surgery may be considered if large breasts are no longer fashionable. Obviously, you may also choose not to invest in a new "look" each season or each year, particularly if a major investment in time, money, or motivation is required. Try to be realistic about what you can and cannot change. If petite women are the rage and you're 5'9", there is little chance you can shrink to fit the fashion of the times. Assessing your true merits and flaws will help you develop a better body image and a sense of confidence; in accepting what you cannot change you may also become more motivated to choose one or two goals you can achieve.

People are often expected to act according to their appearance. The media generally limits itself to showing beautiful people and portraying how they're supposed to act. And according to one study, so-called beautiful people are often perceived as more intelligent, more sexual, and more successful.[18] Some people expect short men to have inferiority complexes and women with glasses to be intellectuals. A man who is big is expected to act rough and tough, while a woman who is small is expected to act helpless. Beautiful women, in particular, frequently find that their appearance dominates other people's perception of them. Susanna explains, "I had many dates who expected me to be all looks and no brains. I was interested in finding a man who appreciated me enough to see beneath the surface, a man who was interested in the other sides of me."

Whatever the current standards are, the inner qualities of a person may be overlooked when appearance is given too much importance. Some people jump to conclusions based on appearance and stay with their first impressions. Others are more open to changing their minds as time goes by. This usually happens when people get to know each other better and are able to discover important aspects about the person which lie beneath the surface.

Exercise: What Image Do You Give Off?

Think back to three recent occasions when you met new people. What first impression did you give? What message do you usually give in your posture, facial expression, clothes, tone of voice, topic of conversation, etc.?

_____

_____

_____

_____

Is there a different impression you would like people to get when they first meet you? If so, what do you need to start doing to make this happen in the future?

_____

_____

_____

_____

If you feel unhappy about the way you look, you need to decide if you're willing to work to change your appearance. To do this, evaluate how you look now and how you want to look in the future. This needs to be done as objectively as possible. Then decide what you specifically need to do to improve your image. Would it require going on a diet, buying a new style of clothing, exercising, trying a new hairstyle, consulting a make-up expert?

For most people, losing weight and getting in shape is first on their list. Some people eat more when tense, bored, depressed, or have nothing better to do. If this pattern is true for you, consider it a cue that you need to change your lifestyle in order to change your weight. You can lose weight if you want to and if you are willing to give yourself time. Overnight changes generally don't work.

Remember, as you consider your possibilities for change, it is important not to compare yourself with others. Ask yourself instead, "Am I the best I can be? Am I paying attention to my appearance and making the most of it?" At every step along the way it is crucial that you congratulate yourself for whatever changes you have made, whether they are minor or major.

Looking Good Is Worth It!

Although there's a lot beneath the surface that you can't display in your looks, you can choose to give a first impression that best fits the image of who you are and who you want to be. People who put extra effort into how they look are more likely to catch someone else's eye.

Subtle Messages

Sometimes people keep potential partners away because they are afraid of what might be expected of them in a close relationship. Their mind-sets lead them to act in certain ways that are bound to affect meetings with potential partners. For instance,

Jim did not want a long-term relationship because he didn't want anyone to try to control his life. "Why should I be coerced into doing things I don't like or want to do? I don't want to lose my freedom. What's more, who knows what kinds of strange habits another person may have? I'm better off by myself."

People who claim they cannot attract anybody no matter how hard they try often give off subtle messages to others to stay away or not get close. They may do this with a condescending look or a distrustful attitude, a critical remark or a silent routine. There are others who smother people with so much "well-meaning" advice that they drive potential partners away. Then there are those who make a positive first impression but later become so needy and draining or possessive and demanding that they end up alone.

Sam complained that his dates backed off from him soon after they got to know him. With some soul-searching, he realized that he often acted charming at first, but after a short time, he would begin to act needy and dependent. Sam would spend much of the time moaning and groaning about how hard his life was. He constantly asked for advice, but when it was given, he would usually turn it down. After a while, his dates would become tired of this and go elsewhere.

Exercise: Do You Keep People Away?

Imagine some friends are sitting around talking about you. How would they describe you? What qualities would they mention if they were trying to arrange a blind date for you?

If they were being critical, what would they say about the way you are when you are meeting new people? Perhaps they would say you talk too much and never listen. Perhaps they would say you expect too much of others. Perhaps they would say you're too bossy or too sloppy. Or perhaps they would say that you tend to stay superficial in conversations, talking only about work or politics but not about yourself. What do you imagine they might say?

Considering their opinions, is there any goal for change you want to set for yourself? If so, what are one or two things you could start doing now?

Be honest with your answers. Bring into awareness what you already know about yourself that will help you target problems and design solutions to get the results you want.

The Wrong Person or the Wrong Place?

Everyone wants to attract the *right* person, yet sometimes they attract the *wrong* one; someone who is too rational or too emotional; too serious or too casual; too pushy or too passive. Who you attract can be determined by the messages you may unintentionally be giving off.

Jeannette, a very energetic, responsible, and attractive woman, complained that nearly every man she met would eventually try to make a pass at her. This included her doctor, her lawyer, her teachers, and "tons of men who are already married." She considered herself an intellectual and a leader. She also knew she liked being noticed but was tired of the kind of attention she got. Her friends pointed out that she was giving sexual come-ons by wearing low-cut dresses and joking with men in overly familiar ways. After considering their comments, she realized they were right and made some changes. By dressing a little more conservatively and acting a little more subdued, she found men treated her with more respect.

Other people are attracted to the wrong partner, even at the first meeting, because they erroneously believe that they can change the other person. Belinda tended to be attracted to men who were strong, silent types. She was intrigued by their strength and unconsciously hoped to find a sweet little boy underneath the hard outer shell. In counseling, Belinda came to realize that she was attracted to men who were actually indifferent and aloof, very much like her father. She hoped she could get them to be tender, as she wished her father had been. Now at 43, after two divorces and one child, she began to figure out how to break out of her pattern.

When people continue to be attracted to partners who are wrong for them, it is often because they are trying to balance the scales of the past and make up for a difficult or unfulfilled relationship they had with one or both of their parents. These people tend to feel that no matter who their current partner is, there may be a more perfect partner out there somewhere. They need to seriously examine their motivations and realize that a partner cannot resolve those kinds of issues for them—only they can.

Some people attract the wrong person because they are looking in the wrong places. For example, in a singles bar most initial contacts are based on physical appearance, social affability, and sexual fantasies. These are frequently superficial encounters that often lead to game-playing and casual sex. Since drinking tends to decrease inhibitions, the spontaneity you witness in other people may not be typical of how they normally are—it may only be a brief intermission. The problem of meeting people in singles bars is compounded by the fear of AIDS and herpes and a lifestyle based on unfulfilling one-night stands. Although going to singles bars may be right for some people, and certainly this is a way of getting out of the house and circulating, they have a garnered a reputation for being "meat markets" and for being a *less* likely place to meet a potential partner. Consequently, singles bars are losing much of their popularity.

Office romances are also common. You may not be thinking of meeting a partner at work, but sometimes it happens. The close contact that comes with working with the same person day in and day out can make the office a fertile ground in which a relationship can take hold.

Office romances sometimes lead to the altar; other times they lead to disaster. If the relationship doesn't work out, the people involved may feel awkward being around each other afterward. For example, Angela, a nurse in a large hospital, noticed a particular doctor was conveniently crossing paths with her most shifts. They got to know each other and started dating, until she realized he wasn't her type. She tried to back off from the relationship politely but he persisted in his pursuit. Finally she got mad and told him off. Subsequently, this made their professional contacts very difficult.

Before you give your heart away, be careful. An office can easily turn into a soap opera, where rumors spread like wildfire and in the end, someone ends up feeling hurt or getting fired.

To check the person out, don't be afraid to ask questions about him or her. Find out everything you can. Trust yourself if you sense there is something you don't like or trust about the person. Remember, you are protecting yourself and your job!

How and Where to Meet Potential Partners

Have you ever asked couples where they first met? Their answers are sometimes surprising, other times fairly common: at a costume party, at the beach, on a volleyball team, at the dentist's office, at an auction, in their own home. As the single population has grown older and more sophisticated, people search for spouses in very creative places and in more direct ways.

You may need to be creative and take a risk in order to create new opportunities to meet people. It's not enough to wait for that moment to happen. You need to get out there and be available and visible to the people you want to meet. To do this, you need to formulate a plan of action and follow it, in a way that is comfortable for you. Here are some important principles that are useful to keep in mind:

1. *Provide yourself with the opportunity to meet other people.*
   For some people, getting out there is easy. Those who are gregarious and involved in numerous activities outside of their work or home life tend to meet people no matter where they are or what they're doing.

   For others, meeting people doesn't come naturally. Their usual complaint is that after working all day, commuting, cooking, and doing chores, there is too little time or energy left to spend socializing. Or they think getting out there is scary and uncomfortable, because they are at a loss to know how to begin a conversation and don't feel confident or assertive when meeting strangers in new places.

You have to decide to make the time to create or utilize opportunities to meet others. Find out about singles programs in your community. Check local newspapers listings of concerts, workshops, lectures, trips, and other activities. Gather information about "safe places" where singles like yourself go. Then gather up your courage and get out there. The more you do it, the more relaxed and confident you'll feel.

2. *Plan your time and follow a regular schedule of activities.* Once you have decided what you want to do, do it on a regular schedule. Following the same pattern helps you meet people, since you will most likely encounter the same people and can more easily strike up conversations with familiar faces—whether it's eating breakfast at the same restaurant at 7:30 A.M. or jogging on the same path at 6:00 P.M., playing tennis or golf every Saturday at eight o'clock or going to church every Sunday at nine. You'll get to know the regulars and be able to spot the newcomers.

   Seeing someone on a regular basis provides a greater chance of becoming friends or lovers. Carol played tennis every Friday night. After doing this for a number of weeks, she got to know many of the other players. Often she would go with them for a drink afterward and, as things turned out, she often sat next to the same man. One night he asked her for a date.

3. *Use your network of friends.* Let them know that you would like to meet some of *their* friends. Group happenings such as barbecues, hikes, birthday parties, and family gatherings can be fun and sometimes hold nice surprises. If your friends set you up with someone who is OK but not the right person for you, don't despair—that person may have a friend who is right for you! If you like to stay home, invite your friends over for a party and tell them to bring some of their friends you don't

know. Like a chain reaction, a friend might just walk in with a man or woman who knocks you off your feet! Remember, your friends can act as your agent, keeping their eyes open for new possibilities.

4. *Get involved in activities you enjoy.* People often meet like-minded souls when involved in activities they enjoy. And they're more likely to be themselves and be less concerned with putting on a facade when doing things they enjoy. At these times, it is easier to strike up a conversation with a stranger because there already is something in common to talk about. For example, Alan often went walking along the beach, bird-watching and daydreaming. Occasionally he would stop and talk to other beachcombers. One day, he met a woman who was a marine biologist. They talked about an environmental impact report she was working on. After that, they met frequently on their walks and went on to form a relationship that led to marriage.

5. *Personal or professional educational activities are a prime meeting ground.* Night courses, weekend seminars, conferences, and special lectures are all high-potential activities for meeting someone with similar interests. The semistructured environment and predictability of contact make educational programs a strong possibility for many people. For example, Peter and Judy were in law school together. They spent hour after hour in the library looking up cases and discussing them. Their meetings, which were a daily occurrence, later developed into friendship, then romance. It seemed natural to them that their relationship became more than an intellectual affair.

6. *Advertise.* Placing an ad in a magazine used to be considered a desperate move, but more and more people are finding it works. (It only has to work once for it to be worth it!) One

study concluded that the most successful ads are those that highlighted the writer's goals and interests and do not have a list of personality requirements.[19] Unsuccessful ads are those that impose various demands or restrictions on the reader. If you decide to advertise, your ad is not the place to include your entire "shopping list." If you are uneasy about meeting people who respond to your ad, an afternoon cup of coffee at a local restaurant is usually a safe way to get acquainted.

Video dating services, another way to meet people, offer better screening than personal ads. If you go to one of these services, you'll be shown a picture album that has both snapshots and brief statements about potential dates, with their interests and hobbies. Then you'll watch brief taped interviews of the people you want to know more about. Any potentials you select are then contacted to come to the dating service's office and review a tape of you. If they are interested in dating you, they are given your phone number. Although unpredictable, video dating services do offer a little more protection than personal ads. Whether or not you get the results you want depends both on the integrity of the service and your willingness to make contact with strangers.

7. *Be alert to possibilities at any moment.* Remember, you may bump into your right partner at any time and any place. In fact, it often happens that people meet someone of their dreams when they are least expecting it. Browsing through a bookstore, wandering through an art gallery, while waiting at the car wash, someone may strike up a conversation that's worth continuing. A grocery store in Cherry Hill, New Jersey capitalized on this desire for safe meeting grounds and offered a "singles night" at the supermarket: "Every Tuesday night, as many as 2,000 men and women wearing name tags check each other out over the broccoli and detergent, hopeful that a magic encounter *in* the aisle could lead them *down* the aisle." In a more highbrow setting, the Smithsonian Institute in

Washington, D.C., arranges evenings where an equal number of single men and women sip champagne and nibble canapés while discussing such topics as Japanese technology and American modern art.[20] Janet Solinger, who arranges these functions, calls it "the squarest singles bar in town."

8. *Have some one-liners ready to start a conversation.* Starting a conversation doesn't require exotic, earth-shaking statements. You can meet someone by simply saying something like:

"Hello, my name is . . .

"Hello, I want to meet you because . . .

"Hello, I notice you are carrying a book I like and . . .

"Hello, you remind me of . . .

"Hello, when I saw you I was . . .

"Hello, could you help me with . . .

"Hello, are you interested in . . .

Having some one-liners already in mind will make it easier to speak up when the right person appears. By striking up conversations with enough people, you will became proficient at making the first contact.

9. *Relax and enjoy the conversation.* Let yourself enjoy meeting people, even if you can tell they are not the partner you are looking for. Don't be overly concerned about how the conversation will go or what you might say when you meet someone. Being self-conscious about what you're saying can make you feel nervous and clumsy. To avoid this, remind yourself that every encounter doesn't have to go perfectly or lead to the altar.

You may feel more relaxed if you remind youself that most people like to talk about themselves and the things they believe in or enjoy doing. So, if you ask new acquaintances questions, they are likely to welcome the chance to express some of their ideas or feelings.

Of course, the same can be true for you. You don't need to share your deep dark secrets the first time you meet someone, but do be willing to talk about yourself, your life, and your opinions.

To enjoy a conversation even more, you need to decide that it's OK to pass time talking about the little things—ideas or events that may seem minor or mundane. These pastimes grease the social wheels by giving people nonthreatening subjects to talk about.

You can't predict or control what someone is going to say to you, so you might as well relax and enjoy the conversation as it develops. Even if you trip over your words or thoughts occasionally, your spontaneity and interest in others will most likely make you more magnetic to them.

10. *Above all, think positively and be yourself!*

Chapter 4

∽∾∞∽

THE DATING GAME

"I've been hurt before, and I'm scared. But I don't want to hide anymore. I want to dance. I want to live. I'm ready. At last, I'm ready to date."

"There was a time in my life when it didn't really matter who I dated. I just wanted to go out and have fun. I cared more for the excitement of the night than for the person I dated. Yet I knew that someone special would come into my life sooner or later. Now it's happened and its wonderful!"

"When I first started dating, I tried desperately to please whomever I was with. That didn't work so I tried playing hard to get. Then I tried to act casual and confident, and even bossy and controlling. At last I discovered that being me was the best approach."

Meeting someone you're interested in is only the first step; the next is to get to know them. This happens as you date. While talking and sharing quiet moments, doing things together, and being around friends and relatives, you find out a lot more about each other, including each other's quirks and eccentricities. As the relationship grows, you may also get into periods of frustration and conflict with each other. This is natural and predictable.

People date for various reasons, including: fun and excitement, convenience, friendship, sex, or to find a mate. In this chapter you will meet the various types of people you might date, such as the Princess or Prince, the Sweetheart and the Teddy Bear, the Incurable Romantic, the Executive Director, and the Casual Lover.

In addition, you will learn some of the more common psychological dating games that people play. You will most likely read about some people you've dated and some of the dating games you've initiated or gotten hooked into. As you read about these styles and games, you will sharpen your skills at getting out of wrong situations and making relationships go more smoothly. All of this will make your dating and selection process easier.

Dating for Fun and Excitement

Some people date only for fun and excitement. They don't want to be in a serious relationship; they don't want dates that lead to long-term commitments. Running on the beach, riding bikes through the hills, going to a good movie or concert, or having a lively party tend to be their style.

Bert explained this point of view, "I like to date several people. I have one friend for dancing, another for skiing, another for scuba diving and another for sharing ideas with. All I want in my life right now is to have fun. I make my intentions known early on. I don't want to get serious and I don't want to hurt anyone."

Dating for Convenience

Some people look for a date who is convenient. They may have tickets to the theater and not want to go alone. They may be invited to the boss's house for a dinner party and are told to bring a date, so they ask a person they think will be satisfactory to the boss. Or they want a tennis partner for a tournament or someone that they can show off so that others will be impressed. Friends may ask them to be a blind date for a visiting cousin or business associate who needs to be accompanied somewhere.

Dating for convenience is common for those who feel embarrassed being single when all their friends are married. Marcy explained her reasons for dating Robert: "It's logical for me to go out with Robert. This way I have someone around to do things with, especially since my married friends seem more comfortable when I'm with a date. I don't want a torrid romance or a serious relationship."

Dating for Companionship

Some people prefer to date people who are friends and are more like brothers and sisters than lovers. As friends, they trust and understand each other and often spend time together sharing ideas, developing projects, and going to events of mutual interest. Some people who date for friendship purposes do not want a commitment; others do.

Don is one who does not. "For a while I dated several women. But soon I got tired of having to put up with their different moods; trying to remember what each one liked was a chore. All I wanted was someone I could enjoy on a regular basis and who shared my interests. Diana is a good friend. We work together and go bowling together. We have been seeing each other for more than eight years. I do not want to get married and she knows it. She'd like something more. But that's the rule of my game and so far she's willing to play according to that rule."

Art took a different position. "I have watched my friends and their romances come and go. Infatuation doesn't last, but a good friend does. A friend is forever. I only date women who know how to be friends. When I do marry, you can be sure it will be to that special friend."

Dating for Sex

Sexual satisfaction is another important reason people date. When dating, most people want to be physically close, to touch and be touched, to hold and be held, to kiss and be kissed. Sexual energies are often ignited. The most pleasurable sexual experiences take place when emotional *and* physical needs are satisfied by mutual consent.

Unfortunately, sex is an area in which exploitation can occur. One partner may act seductive and manipulate a partner into having sex. Someone else, instead of acting seductive, may demand sex on the first date as if saying, "Don't expect to see me again if you're not willing to go to bed with me."

"Recreational sex," the tidal wave of the '60s and '70s, has fallen into ill repute in the '80s. With the advent of the birth control, such as the pill, sex became a sport. But with the spread of herpes and AIDS, people have become more cautious. In addition, many have decided that casual sex doesn't really make life more fun. It often makes things complicated or leads to a dead end, where relationships are shallow and unsatisfying. After a night of rolling in the hay or a month of passionate motel encounters, it is too easy to end up feeling disappointed and bored. Recreational sex doesn't necessarily lead to a good relationship.

Sexual mind-sets can enhance a relationship or can become a burden to it. If your sexual mind-sets are too permissive, you won't know how to say no when you want to. If your mind-sets are too rigid, you may hold yourself back from being close to someone you love, and feel tortured by your natural desires. People with healthy mind-sets can feel comfortable exploring the sexual aspects of a relationship with the right partner. If your mind-sets are well balanced, you'll know what is right for you when you are with your right partner. Healthy sexual mind-sets can help you find a path through the labyrinth of sexual choices and decisions you will encounter while dating.

Dating for Psychological Compensation

People often look for dates who will compensate for their psychological shortcomings and give them what they have never had in a relationship. Someone who is passive may date someone who is strong and independent and will make all the decisions. Someone who feels starved for affection may date someone who is nurturing and willing to act like a mother or father. Someone who distrusts people may pick a partner who is a loner and won't expect much intimacy.

Louise liked the safety and security her boyfriend provided. "Charles is the oldest in his family. He always took care of his younger brothers and sisters. Every time we go out, he takes good care of me. I feel safe when I'm around him. I don't have to worry about anything. I've never really been taken care of before, so it's nice to have him in my life."

Dating to Find a Mate

People who date to find a mate aren't generally interested in wasting their time or going around in circles with a series of wrong partners. They carefully pick and chose where to go to meet someone.

For them, it's important to find out what their date is *really* like. They want to see beyond first impressions and façades. They want to learn about the other person's dreams and mind-sets, and especially to find out if their values coincide. For example, people who enjoy certain kinds of sports, politics, business, or religion often want a partner with similar values. So they look for them at a sporting event, a political meeting, a business conference, or a religious gathering.

For those who want to find a mate, dating provides an opportunity to observe each others' unique ways of dealing with different situations. Each may notice the others' ways of solving problems, expressing thoughts, showing tenderness and affection, even ways of solving conflict. Noticing how he relates to people or how she acts under pressure gives them a chance to discover if they want to pursue the relationship or not. If they have sex, it gives them an opportunity to find out if their sexual energies and values are compatible.

The Reasons You Date

Your reasons for dating may vary from time to time as your circumstances and partners change. The obvious goal is to find dates with essentially the same motivations as yours. The best way to do this is to talk about it with each other. Let your date know what you like about being with him or her. Ask your date for his or her opinions on dating. This conversation can give you more indicators for the probable direction of your relationship in the future.

Personality Styles and the Dating Games
People Play

People have various ways they attract and treat a date. Their personal style and approach frequently determine their success in meeting, dating, and maintaining a relationship. Although each person is unique, people tend to act in similar ways when dating.

There are a number of common personality types you may encounter when dating. Obviously some will be more attractive to you than others. Occasionally people do not readily recognize each others' styles, because they are enchanted by their dreams of the ideal partner or mesmerized or blinded by their mind-sets. To find the right partner, you need to discover what style of person you like best, and to choose your dates consciously.

Each personality style has its strengths, yet each also has a tendency to lead to specific psychological games if that style is overdone and carried to its extreme.[21] Whatever the personality type, all people play psychological games with each other from time to time. Psychological games involve a series of predictable transactions that eventually lead to one or both people not feeling OK in the end. People play psychological games because they don't know how to get their needs met openly and honestly. Games are indirect, often unconscious, ways to get something we want or need.[22] Sometimes these games are mild and only bothersome to the relationship; sometimes they are intense and destructive to it.

Some people date without getting into games. They handle things in a fairly straightforward manner—communicating openly and honestly and retaining an awareness of their needs, desires, and motivations. Others seem to slip into a predictably frustrating pattern when under stress, when the relationship is moving too fast, starts getting too close, or when things aren't going their way. A few people get caught in more than one game, which can make the relationship fairly chaotic.

The following is a review of several of the more common personality styles and a favored game someone with that style is likely to play. As you read these, bear in mind that a game is not restricted to only one personality type—anyone can play it—but you are more likely to encounter certain games with matching personality styles. Also presented are practical suggestions for avoiding games before they start, or for stopping them after you've recognized them. By understanding these common games you will better understand both yourself and your potential partners. The styles and games presented are only a sampling; a full review would be encyclopedic. Those presented include:

The Personality Style	*A Game They Might Play*
The Princess or Prince	The Hard to Get Game
Sweethearts and Teddy Bears	The Indecision Game
The Incurable Romantic	The Jealousy Game
The Casual Lover	The Indifferent Game
The Executive Director	The Controlling Game

The Princess or Prince

These people feel important and special. Success, beauty, prestige, or love are constantly on their minds. They like to be the center of attention and to be admired. Like a prince or princess, they need an audience. They expect people to favor them and tell them "You're wonderful!" and feel angry when they don't.

Princes and Princesses are very discriminating and selective about whom they date. Their dream is to have a partner who is the best of the best, and they will not settle for anything less if they can help it. They like to date someone who is a suitable escort when seen in public; therefore they are often especially concerned with their partner's looks. They can be critical of others and see them as not good enough, or they want others to prove their worth. They may seem indifferent or stuck up, because they wait for others to start the conversation and are polite and proper in their replies. They are attracted to dates who admire them and consider them sophisticated and hard to get.

For example, William is a man nobody would dream of calling "Bill." He is named after his father and grandfather and often uses the roman numeral III after his name. It is not unusual for him to talk about his family lineage. He's widely traveled and well educated. Because he is very well off financially, he is often invited as an extra man to dinner parties by hostesses who imagine he would be just right for their best friend. However once at the party, William is the type who is hard to get to know. He says all the right things and is polite to everyone, but it is impossible to find out what is really going on behind his proper façade. This becomes a challenge many women find attractive.

The Hard to Get Game

Some people, like the Princess or Prince, start out hard to get and end up hard to please. At first, their dates may find them mysterious and intriguing. They feel charmed and challenged by their elusiveness and want to conquer them. Others may want to serve them, catering to their whims with a litany of "Yes, dear." But once in a relationship, the Prince or Princess is often demanding. Because there is room for only one star on center stage, they may act self-centered, competitive, or (in the case of the Princess) discounting to keep others off stage. Not willing to let a partner be equally important nor able to appreciate the value of real heart-to-heart connection, this person may eventually end up alone.

If you're dating someone who plays hard to get, you can get things on a better course, if you:

- Don't fall for their façade.

- Maintain your own sense of identity.

- Be kind and considerate but not self-deprecating.

- Express your point of view clearly and don't back off or let the other person put you down.

If you recognize yourself as a Prince or Princess who tends to play hard to get, you may be keeping yourself from a good relationship. Consider the following suggestions:

- Learn to validate and appreciate other ways of doing things.

- Let your partner have center stage time, too.

- Learn to let down your guard with more people.

- Be willing to talk about your personal doubts and dreams so your partner can get to know you at a deeper level and appreciate what makes you tick.

- Let others be in charge, especially when you are going out to do something fun together.

- Learn to say you're sorry and mean it.

Sweethearts and Teddy Bears

Sweethearts and Teddy Bears are polite, considerate, friendly, and "lovable." They try hard and mean well. They enjoy themselves and their dates in a relaxed and cozy way. This is the kind of person who is easy to be around, even though he or she is a bit low on passion and excitement. Some like to stay home and read or work on a hobby, others like to go for a long drive as much as or more than going to a party. They are often about twenty pounds overweight—just right for hugging and snuggling up to.

Sweethearts and Teddy Bears tend to be very responsible and act like nurturing parents. They often feel uncomfortable without something to do and most comfortable when they are taking care of others. They will often initiate conversations and make strangers feel at home just by their warm hello. They try to be the right person in the right place at the right time. They are fast thinkers and have great intuition, so much so that they are often masters at reading other people's facial expressions and nonverbal cues. When their dates are unhappy, they immediately try to make things better. They are very understanding of a partner's problems and are always ready to take the blame when something goes wrong. In an argument, they can be volatile one moment and apologetic the next. They forgive and forget easily.

Connie is a Sweetheart. She is fairly attractive, though she wears little makeup and dresses simply. She goes to her aerobics classes every morning before work. She doesn't have a lot of friends, but the ones she has, she has known for many years. Her friends often come to her with their tales of woe; she listens and gives advice that is seldom confrontational and usually boils down to "wait and see what happens." Connie dates occasionally and when on a date, she is talkative but never noisy or boisterous, as if she's worried she might do or say something wrong. She tends to attract men who are the strong and silent types because of her warm, nurturing, and nonintrusive way.

Ben is a Teddy Bear. He is often called "Gentle Ben" and is a true gentleman in the best sense of the word. Ben always has a friendly word for anyone he meets and is usually in the same optimistic mood. He is a hard worker but somehow doesn't get caught in the rat race. He goes at a constant even pace—not too fast, not too slow. He keeps up on current events, so he is always able to carry on a lively conversation. He prefers a simple life and likes to go to the same restaurants and to take familiar drives. With women, Ben is like a knight in shining armor. He likes to save them from hardship and is willing to slay dragons to protect any damsel he is dating. His rescues usually work.

The Indecision Game

Nurturing people, like the Sweethearts and Teddy Bears, often have trouble knowing what they want for themselves because they've spent so much time catering to what other people want. Yet there comes a time when they have to make decisions, and that's when things get difficult.

The indecision game is often played by someone who is dating more than one person or has a new love but is still getting out of a previous marriage. Trying to keep everyone happy and not hurt anyone, this person may feel pulled in both directions between two lovers and think, "What if I make the decision and I'm not happy or it doesn't work out? I'll end up alone. I really can't take that risk. I don't want to hurt anybody. I'm really a good person and I'm trying hard to find out what's the best solution for everybody. I wish others would be patient a little while longer." These people often agonize over making the final decision. The more they are pressured, the more they are unable to decide; they act confused and feel stuck. The longer they are indecisive, the more they feel guilty and depressed. When someone finally demands action, Sweethearts and Teddy Bears either give in or they give up and get out of the relationship. Either way, they don't feel good about their decision.

If you're dating someone who can't make up their mind about your relationship:

- Make your own decision. Don't leave it up to your partner.

- Establish a date by which *you* will decide what to do if your partner hasn't taken action and gotten results.

- Get your partner to clarify what he/she is specifically waiting for.

- Assume your partner cannot make the decision to be with you, if the indecision continues. Decide if you are willing to put up with this indecisiveness or if it distresses you enough to end the relationship.

If you see yourself as a Sweetheart or Teddy Bear and are indecisive about a relationship:

- Pay attention to your reasons for not wanting to take action. Your reasons might be a warning worth heeding.

- Be willing to say what's true instead of acting as if you're stuck.

- Set a deadline for yourself.

- Get the minor issues out of the way, so the major ones can be decided more easily.

The Incurable Romantic

Some people can't help but be romantics at heart, even when their realistic side is in charge. Incurable Romantics are dedicated to creating a loving world. They usually have high energy and are willing to go for what they want. While dating, they often spend time planning to make their time together memorable. Anticipation adds to their excitement.

Incurable Romantics prefer an exclusive relationship and have a strong need to be special to someone. When they meet the right person, they fall in love with their whole heart. They usually proceed with a deep feeling of optimism in spite of the bruises they may carry from past relationships. Their love relationship becomes their top priority and they are willing to overcome any obstacles to make it work.

Incurable Romantics tend to be fun and emotionally expressive. They are passionate and poetic, sexual and sensuous. They pay attention to details and little things mean a lot to them. When someone says the right words, Incurable Romantics often melt. On the surface they can be fun and independent, yet underneath they often are afraid of being abandoned and have a strong need to be taken care of. Consequently, they may want to hear "I love you" many times a day.

Roxanne is an Incurable Romantic. Flying home from a business meeting, she met Greg and was immediately attracted to him. The following week they went out for dinner and ended up talking nearly half the night. She was astounded at how easy it was to talk with him. She was enchanted by his openness and concern for other people. More fun-filled weekends and romantic evenings followed. Soon Greg became her central interest in life and her friends never saw her without him. Being an Incurable Romantic, she would call and leave funny messages on his answering machine and send him romantic cards in the mail. Once she surprised him by sending a dozen roses to his office. She believed in expressing her excitement rather than acting casual or playing hard to get. She tried to keep the relationship in perspective so as not to feel let down if it didn't work out, but secretly she couldn't help having high hopes for it. Even though they had only known each other for two months, she was already thinking many years in the future.

Incurable Romantics love excitement. Their relationships tend to be intense and emotional. Wanting life to be meaningful and passionate, they often go through highs and lows trying to keep their love intense all the time. In an argument, they may get explosive or melodramatic, then want to kiss and make up and act as if the fight never happened. Being deeply committed to a relationship, their loyalty is high and their willingness to hang in there is a major asset.

The Jealousy Game

One of the most common games that Incurable Romantics can fall into is the Jealousy Game. Jealousy used to be a popular part of romance; it still is in some cultures. In the United States, however, jealousy is often considered childish and overly dramatic. Instead, people are expected to be independent and not be bothered by qualms of doubt about infidelity.

Jealousy comes from the natural desire to be special to someone and to have an exclusive relationship. The word *jealousy* comes from the word *zealot*, which means to be highly committed, active, and loyal to a cause. Jealousy and envy are closely related. When feeling jealousy, a person has love but is afraid of losing it; when feeling envy, a person doesn't have love and wants it.

There are many kinds of jealousy. Most commonly, people are jealous of another person's affections or potential attractiveness, ("I saw you flirting with her!"). Lovers also get jealous of the time and attention their partner gives to other people, ("You treat your kids better than you treat me!"), and of the time the partner spends in other activities or interests, ("Your career is more important to you than I am!") Some jealousy is normal. Many people act a little bit jealous to show their love for each other. But some people overdo it.

As an emotional power play, jealousy can be used to manipulate a partner into being more attentive, romantic, tender, and reassuring. Lovers also act jealous as a way to hold on to what they've got. It is as if they believe that by being angry and demanding loyalty they will be able to keep a tight rein on their partner and make sure he or she is not looking around at others: "I can't trust you because you're weak, fickle and gullible and could easily be seduced. And I can't trust other men [women] who are more attractive or magnetic than I. They're too devious and conniving, and only want to take you away from me. So you'd better not give them a chance!"

Jealousy can come from a deep sense of inadequacy and a fear of being replaced. It can be a reaction to a real situation or it can be a projection of an imagined fantasy; in either case, it can become an obsession. In fact jealousy in the extreme is love gone wild.

When jealousy gets out of hand, people overreact to minor events, have irrational and angry outbursts or tantrums. When they explode, they may be more than mad—they can be verbally and physically abusive. When the partner has finally had enough abuse and is ready to walk out, the jealous one may make suicidal threats to force the partner into staying and submitting.

If your partner acts too jealous and you find your relationship is suffering because of it, you may need to:

- Establish expectations of behavior you will both abide by. Make sure you both accept these expectations. Do not accept restrictions your partner tries to put on you unless you believe in them too.

- Share your friends and activities with your partner.

- Limit the number of reassurances you will give your partner each day. Remember your partner feels insecure and needs some reassurance but that too much will only reinforce his/her attitude.

- Have a signal your partner can give you when he or she wants reassurance and doesn't want to play the jealousy game to get it.

- Get out of the relationship temporarily and get some relationship counseling together, if the fighting gets too intense or too frequent.

If you are an Incurable Romantic who tends to be the jealous type and are ready and willing to break this pattern, you can:

- Be clear on what you want and expect from your partner. Talk it over and agree on what are fair and reasonable standards of behavior for you both.

- Do things to improve your self-esteem and to learn to trust other people. That way you won't imagine or fear the worst is happening.

- Build a bigger world for yourselves with more activities and friends, sometimes as a couple, other times on your own.

- Plan and enjoy frequent romantic times together so you won't have to fight to get them.

The Casual Lover

Casual people tend to feel good about themselves and others. They do not seem to worry about whether or not they will meet someone. Casual people are often self-confident. They are sure of themselves, trustworthy, and welcome new friends because they are easy to be with and wear well with time. They tend to keep away from people who act like surrogate parents to them.

Their sense of romance comes naturally; they don't seem to work hard to make things happen. Relaxed and easygoing, the Casual Lover lives by a noncompetitive philosophy of love—everybody can win, there's enough to go around.

Raymond slides into a room and looks over the situation in a very confident way. Everything about him is casual; the way he walks, talks, dresses, acts, and approaches people. He is very confident about himself and has an attitude that if it happens, it happens and if it doesn't happen now, it will sooner or later. He enjoys dancing and is good looking. Furthermore, he knows it, but doesn't let it go to his head. Instead he is actually a bit shy at first. At a party, he can always be seen laughing and talking to strangers. If there's a guitar around, he's soon playing some light tunes and others frequently join in singing. He is so comfortable and relaxed, others feel safe approaching him—and many women do.

The Indifferent Game

People who are casual and confident can be so much fun and so easy to be with that they have a magnetic pull to them. But some people go overboard with this attitude. They are so casual and confident that they become indifferent to their partner's dreams of love. For them, early dating is often fun and passionate, but when their partner shows signs of wanting more of a future together, the Casual Lover's indifference comes out and he or she refuses to make any long-term commitment.

If the partner is willing to keep things at a close friendship, the relationship can go on comfortably for years. But if the partner wants more, the Casual Lover will usually back out with a sigh of resignation.

If you are dating someone who is too casual about your relationship:

- Get clear on his/her personal goals and time schedule and find out if he/she wants to get into a serious relationship or not.

- Work with your partner to become more tolerant and understanding of emotions.

- Teach him/her how to be more nurturing.

- Don't be willing to wait too long and let time and other potential partners pass you by.

If you are a Casual Lover, confident of your ability to survive but are afraid of getting into a committed relationship, you can:

- Discern whether your indifference is because of your partner or because of a more general disinterest you have in being in a long-term relationship.

- Understand that most people are looking for something more and do not like their dreams played with, so make sure early on that your date knows your intentions and relationship boundaries.

- Stop worrying about whether you will be hurt again. All relationships have some painful moments, but good relationships have far more pleasurable ones. Take a risk at living with more emotional depth again.

- Begin to let yourself dream of what a good relationship would be for you and let yourself believe you can have it if you try. Set your sights on the future.

The Executive Director

People who are assertive and like to be in charge of things often pride themselves on being objective, rational, strong, and predictable. They are deeply committed to their values and are headstrong, even stubborn. They try to have a logical reason for everything they do and they prefer to rely on themselves. They are inspiring because of their high standards and their willingness to work hard. They expect other people to be either independent or compliant and will motivate and push a partner to do more. By being results-oriented, they often gain power and prestige.

Many such people are straightforward and direct. They don't want to waste their time or lead others on. They want to avoid hassles and problems. By acting like the captain of the ship, they attract dates or partners who admire their strength and clarity of mind.

David tends to take charge. Called for jury duty, he became the jury foreman. At the company picnic, he gets people and activities organized and going. At a party, he's always in the center of the conversation. When he pays attention to women, they are often flattered and responsive. And when he is without a date, women often find very creative excuses to make contact with him.

The expectation of many Executive Directors is that everything will go well according to their plans. But inwardly they fear that they may lose control of the situation. They like to work intensely and expect their work to be perfect. Pleasure and interpersonal relationships come second for them. Even on weekends when loved ones are playing, they usually need to be doing something productive. They have to have a strong justification in order to let themselves relax.

They express feelings of warmth and tenderness to a few people close to them. But even those close to them are required to be loyal and submit to their way of doing things. When under fire, they tend to clam up and withdraw into their thoughts, leaving others wondering where they went. Since they often lack awareness of others' feelings and the problems elicited by their attitude, they are often perceived as cold and unemotional or bossy. When criticized about how they act, they are ready to counterattack and prove they are right.

People who like to be in control too much will often pick a partner they can dominate, someone who will nod yes and obey them. Or they will pick someone as an antidote to their rigidity, someone who is relaxed, knows how to have fun, and takes life more casually. Occasionally they pick someone who has a similar personality, who also strives for the leadership role, perfection, and who can be content with a ritualistic, intellectual relationship. The Executive Director will attract partners who are looking for the strength, structure, and security they offer.

The Controlling Game

A person who originally is attracted to an Executive Director will often feel secure at first, but after a while will feel bored by the Executive Director's self-righteousness or rigidity. It is common for the partner of an Executive Director to try to act pleasing and get approval. Yet after a while, the partner may act highly emotional to defend against the Executive Director's continuous logical control. The partner may try to get the Executive Director to ease up on the controls by pressuring him/her to take a vacation, to talk about personal matters, to express emotions, to relax, etc. But that may not work. In the end, the partner may lose interest and instead look for romantic contact elsewhere.

If you're dating someone who has to be in control of everything, there are several steps you can take to make things different:

- Make sure you have regularly scheduled time alone together, not talking about business or family matters, so you can talk about playful, romantic, or emotional concerns.

- Agree to have frequent brief conversations rather than long intense ones.

- Require him or her to respect your feelings, opinions, and points of view.

- Teach your partner to identify feelings internally and in others and to recognize hidden ways of expressing them. Reinforce your partner for every positive and open expression of feelings.

If you are too controlling, here are some things you can do to change:

- Learn to appreciate other people's feelings and opinions. You don't always have to have the last word.

- Accept that your partner has other ways of seeing and doing things that are as valid as yours.

- Learn to talk about your feelings, especially your doubts and inadequacies.

- Learn to give honest compliments. Don't discount or criticize others, and when you do, learn to say you're sorry and mean it.

- Let others be in charge sometimes, especially when you are doing something fun together.

- Learn to relax using biofeedback, meditation, long walks, or quiet music.

Exercise: Your Dating Style

Now that you have reviewed these various personality styles and approaches to dating, think back to some people you've dated. On the following page list them by name. What were their personality styles? (You can use those mentioned or invent your own.)

Person	Personality Style
_____	_____
_____	_____
_____	_____
_____	_____
_____	_____
_____	_____
_____	_____

As you look at the list, do you notice any pattern? Do you tend to pick one kind of personality or several? Have your tastes evolved in some way?

_____

_____

_____

_____

What is your personality style and approach and how has it matured over the years?

_____

_____

_____

_____

What personality style do you find most attractive and compatible now and why?

_____
_____
_____
_____
_____
_____
_____
_____
_____
_____

Exercise: Unraveling the Dating Games You've Played

Again list the people you've dated. What game(s), if any, did you get into with each one?

Person	The Game(s) We Got Into
_____	_____
_____	_____
_____	_____
_____	_____
_____	_____
_____	_____
_____	_____

Do you tend to get into the same games with most people you date or do certain personality styles bring out different responses in you?

_____

_____

_____

_____

_____

_____

_____

_____

_____

Which games have you learned to avoid and which ones might you get caught up in in future relationships?

_____

_____

_____

_____

_____

_____

_____

_____

_____

What do you think are your unmet needs that lead to the games you get into? How might you get these needs met more directly?

The Game	The Unmet Need	A More Direct Approach
_____	_____	_____
_____	_____	_____
_____	_____	_____
_____	_____	_____
_____	_____	_____

Avoiding the dating games people play is not always easy, but it is always worth it. The best way to do this is to be clear, both with yourself and with your partner, on what you want and how that affects your behavior. When something doesn't feel right, slow down and talk about it until you feel resolved about it. If no resolution occurs, then use the impasse as a possible warning flag signaling you to proceed with extra caution.

Smart Dating

There are many more personality styles that you may meet from time to time, each with a game they have a tendency to play. You may have already known a Quiet and Shy type who ended up in a Dependency Game, a Workaholic who played a Too Busy Game, a Best Friend whose relationships seemed to follow a Going Nowhere Special pattern, or a Flirt whose Disappearing Act left people feeling used.

As you begin to look closer at the people you date, enjoy the strengths of their personality styles and consider in advance what might be the games they might fall into. Keep in mind that every couple will play some games from time to time.

Worthwhile relationships are the ones in which both people are willing to shift gears and do something to pull themselves out of painful traps they get into. Most important, acknowledging these same patterns in yourself will let you enjoy your differences in style.

First impressions and first dates can provide some opportunity to cull out partners who are obviously not right for you. But those early encounters may not give you all the knowledge you need about each other. To increase your chances of picking the right partner (and of not getting stuck with the wrong one), you need to use a more precise screening technique: a gradual but extensive interview.

Chapter 5

ဢဢ

INTERVIEWING
THE RIGHT PARTNER

*"In the last couple of years I've been seriously
interested in three different women. The
problem is I've made some poor decisions and
have been burned. I'm ready to try again, but
I wish I knew how to make a better choice."*

*"I just met someone who might turn out to
be the one. I think it could become a great
romance but I'm just getting started in my
career and I don't know if I should get so
involved at this time."*

*"I keep waiting for some sign or signal that
tells me, 'This is it!' I don't think that's smart
of me but what else can I do?"*

It's natural and normal to be selective, to want to find the right
partner and build a relationship that lasts. Some people actively
search for the right person. Others just sit and wait for someone
wonderful to come along. There are a few who are willing to take
almost anyone just to avoid being alone.

Instead of luck, patience, or haphazard actions, it's time to try a
new approach that is sensible, effective, and fun. After meeting a
good potential partner, it is smart to ask some very particular
questions to ascertain if the two of you could be compatible. You
need to decide in advance, *before you give your heart away*, what
the other person is really like.

In this chapter, you will find a way to get to know someone very well. This chapter shows you how to "interview" a potential partner to find out if he or she is right for you. Some basic considerations about interviewing are covered, such as the importance of mutual self-disclosure and dialogue rather than one-sided investigation. More important, the chapter contains specific questions for you to use to get to know the other person in-depth, and brief explanations of the reasoning behind each question. Also presented is a system for understanding the various sides of someone's personality which you will discover while dating and interviewing the person.

You need to find out, now, the behavior and personality you can expect to encounter later. And the sooner you can find this out, the better! If you find out as much as you can at the beginning, you can be prepared, informed, and protected against a wrong or painful choice. Of course, no matter how carefully you screen someone, there will be surprises. With any luck, they will be pleasant ones!

Interviewing Concepts

Selecting potential partners can be compared to the selection process in the job market. Before being hired, people usually go through a series of interviews. Smart applicants also interview the boss or company representative to see if the job will be right for them if it is offered.

This concept of a reciprocal interview can be applied when interviewing a potential partner. Part of the joy of getting to know someone is letting that person get to know you. Talking about past adventures and future ambitions can be fun as well as informative. In fact, two of the favorite topics of conversation between dating couples are past experiences and plans for the future.

In a job interview, the employer asks specific questions to gain relevant knowledge of the applicant. A random "get acquainted" process would be inefficient and leave too many gaps in information. This principle can be applied to the search for the right partner as well.

How do you get to know another person in a short time? How do you ask about important matters without seeming invasive or nosey? How do you gather information without behaving like an investigative reporter? How can you interpret the information and avoid inaccurate conclusions? How can you get an accurate and balanced picture of the other person's strengths and weaknesses?

In return, how can you let the other person know about you without bragging of your successes or confessing to your failures? How can you avoid sounding like a historian or a dreamer while sharing those aspects of yourself that add depth to the total picture of who you are? And how can the conversations be a joy rather than a job?

These questions are important and need practical answers. Later in this chapter a series of questions are presented that you can use to find out many of the crucial facts about the other person which you need to know to make a smart choice. They are meant to be used as a general guide, not as a recipe or computer program to be followed exactly. Once you have reviewed the procedure, you can decide which questions would be useful for you to use and which ones would not.

Exercise: Getting Ready with Imagery

Imagery is a very effective tool. Here it involves "seeing" a situation as it could be and listening to words that might be said. For a moment, imagine two people sitting talking to each other. For a business interview, they would probably be sitting on opposite sides of a desk asking and answering questions. But in this fantasy, imagine that they are on a date. You are one of the people and your current "potential" is your date. The two of you might be walking down the street or sitting over a cup of coffee. Your conversation will be more free-flowing than a job interview because it takes place informally, at various times, in various situations, and in pieces rather than all at once. Instead of completing a long questionnaire about vital and not-so-vital statistics, questions are asked informally in the context of the conversation. Questions need not be prying or intrusive. They can be amusing: "What was the most embarrassing thing that happened to you when you were little?" or meaningful: "What do you value most in life?" Spend a few minutes visualizing yourself in this kind of situation.

Be clear on what you really want to find out about a potential partner. See and hear yourself with the other person. Plan an interview in your imagination. Figure out your priorities, so you can pay attention to the things that really matter as you get to know each other. In doing this, your logical self can function as an ally to insure that you don't get carried away by the part of you that may be enchanted and in a daze.

Picking the Time and Place

Sharing information happens naturally for many people. They talk freely about their experiences. For others with painful experiences or with strong beliefs about being private, they may not want to talk about those times, or may have even forgotten many events in an effort to blunt the pain.

If you keep your mind alert, you can discover important things about the other person at almost any time or place. However, the place or situation sometimes dictates the topic of conversation. An extreme example might be an office party. This is not the time to ask someone about their ambitions or dissatisfactions with their job. But over dinner, this topic could lead to a real dialogue and a shared intimacy.

You might feel comfortable talking about your dreams for the future while taking a long drive with a date, but not at a crowded, noisy concert. It's often necessary to give the dialogue a relaxed time and space to develop. You need to sense the mood of the day and of the other person. He or she may not be as in touch with their feelings and values as you are. Also, the other person may not know yet whether or not you can be trusted with confidences.

What to Look for

Knowing what to look for will make getting acquainted a lot easier. Many theories have been devised to try to explain what makes people tick. Each theory is like a different map, showing special points of interest and what to look for along the way. Maps of the personality also outline different aspects of people. Each psychological theory has its own special way of describing the personality. The descriptions are to help people understand themselves and others, why people do what they do, and how their thoughts and feelings affect their behavior.

Transactional Analysis (TA) is a psychological theory that provides one such map that can make the journey of getting to know someone much easier.[23] It will not point out every possible thing to notice along the way. No map can. But it will make some aspects of yourself and the other person much more understandable. Using TA can make the interviewing process easier and the answers easier to understand.

Three Things We All Have in Common

Everyone has different facets of their personality. Yet according to TA, there are three parts of personality that everyone has: the child part, the adult part, and the parent part. Everyone acts like a child at times. This is called the "Child ego state" or the "inner Child." It is the little girl or little boy within each person that continues to live on far beyond childhood. In the child ego state are the memories, thoughts, and mind-sets formed in early childhood, as well as learned habits and behaviors.

The Child is experienced inwardly and expressed outwardly. The inner Child can be heard in people's voices when they laugh, complain, or worry. It can be seen in their posture and facial expression, when they are bent over in sadness or smiling with excitement. It can be heard in their words when they are exaggerating ("She's the most fantastic woman in the world!"), complaining ("Why doesn't he call when he says he's going to?") feeling passionate ("Your kisses drive me crazy!") or feeling desperate ("I can't take this anymore.").

Feelings and emotions are the special realm of the inner Child. A person's Child can be charming and fun, excited and intense, heartbroken and sad, or lonely and depressed. It may be energized or tired, curious or bored, self-centered or compassionate. It's the Child in us that wants what it wants when it wants it.

The Child in us expresses feelings, thoughts, and behaviors that all children have. Even more, each person's unique ways of thinking and acting when little are still alive within and surface frequently. The little boy or little girl in a person often comes out in the dating process with the excitement of meeting someone new or the disappointment of a relationship coming to an end.

Have you ever noticed childlike behavior in yourself and others and wondered about it? For example, have you ever heard couples talking baby talk to each other? Have you ever been so excited you couldn't sit still when you were about to go on a date with someone you really liked? Have you ever felt lonely and heard yourself crying, sobbing, or weeping in your head the way a little child cries when he or she is unhappy? This childlike part of personality is the Child ego state.

The second personality characteristic all people have in common is the "Parent ego state" or "inner Parent." Each person carries around in their head some of the values, opinions, and behaviors learned from their parents and parent-surrogates. For instance, if someone's parents were honest, that person is also probably honest and will encourage and value honesty in others. If a person's parents were bossy, then the person will likely act bossy toward others, or expect others to boss him or her.

Parental opinions, to a large part, make up the "shoulds" and "ought tos" that people live by. These shoulds and ought tos form the foundation of people's values, attitudes, and expectations about life.

Parental opinions show up especially in discussions regarding how to raise children, how to spend money, politics, religion, who should make final decisions, and who's right. Parental behaviors often may be seen when people are taking care of others or showing them how to do things.

People not only parent children; they also act like parents toward their partner. They may do this when their partner comes home from a hard day at work, when she is down or discouraged, or when he is asking for reassurance or advice. People with healthy parent models will know how to respond to these situations appropriately, with an effective balance of love and support. People with overnurturing parents will probably act overnurturing toward their partner or spouse. If your parents were aloof and distant, you may act that way with friends and lovers.

In addition to the inner Child and Parent ego states, everyone has the ability to think logically on the basis of facts and information, to identify and analyze what's going on, and to act in ways appropriate to the situation. This third part of the personality is called the "Adult ego state." It is not related to a person's age. Rather, it is the part of people that collects data objectively, thinks clearly, and makes decisions based on facts and information instead of on Parent traditions and Child feelings.

The Adult is logical and rational, but that does not mean it ignores emotions and feelings. Rather, it puts all the necessary elements into perspective. The Adult makes decisions based on accurate information while also taking into account the teachings and values of the Parent and the wants, needs, and feelings of the Child.

People need to use their Adult as the one in charge of their decisions and actions. The Adult needs to function like a grown-up might around children, giving friendly supervision, making occasional interventions, yet fully in charge when there are important decisions to be made.

According to TA theory, when you meet someone, you are not just meeting one person, you are meeting several people in one. What seems to be a meeting of just two people ends up being a meeting of six or more—your Child, your Parent, and your Adult and his or her Child, Parent, and Adult. No wonder getting to know someone can get to be a challenge!

Therefore, if you want to get to know the person well, you need to interview each of the characters in their personality, as well as let them know about your different facets. Knowing people have three basic components to their personalities can lend some structure to the interview process. By interviewing each part, you can make better sense of what you are learning about the other person.

The interview is designed to provide your Adult with abundant information so you can make a discerning decision regarding who to date or possibly who to marry. It would be foolish to make such a decision based solely on the logic of a child. And you're probably not interested in having your parents decide who you are going to date. Only an informed Adult will give you the capacity to make this decision more wisely. You need to do this *before* you fall helplessly and hopelessly in love.

Interviewing the Inner Child

The Child ego state is the part of the personality that, for some people, is most closely involved in meeting, dating, and falling in love. It is the Child that dreams of a better life and feels hopeful of meeting the right person.

When the Child comes out, it can be fun, as when a person is playing in the waves at the beach or laughing at a good joke. But it can be bothersome when a person is acting self-centered in an argument and refuses to listen to other points of view or yells accusations that do not make sense.

This part of the personality can be so strong at times that the more rational parts of a person may be overruled by the Child's emotions. For example, when people first fall in love, sometimes they can't concentrate on their work. Or when they want to spend money on clothes, gifts, trips, cars, etc., they sometimes do it even though they can't afford it. It's the Child that lives on credit card delusions. In both cases, the Child's feelings and fantasies are so active that the Adult needs to intervene.

Getting to know about a person's inner Child is probably the easiest and most fun part of the interview. It occurs naturally as people talk and do things together. There are several topics of conversations that will invite a person's Child onstage.

"What do you like to do for fun?" What people do for fun is a good indicator of how they will act in a relationship. Someone who has a variety of hobbies and interests will likely have a diversity of topics to talk about. Someone who is athletic will likely want to have sports as an important part of their relationship. Someone who loves to read three novels a week may prefer intellectual or cultural activities. Someone who tends to be a workaholic may not take time to play with you once the romance wears off.

Questions to discover more about a person's preferences and style of having fun can include: *"What did you do for fun when you were little?* Did you play indoors or out? Did you play with other kids or by yourself?"* Childhood patterns of play often set the mold for later play activities. For example, one man who grew up playing outdoors on the hills behind his house spent most of his play time as an adult hiking and photographing nature. These activities were familiar to him. He found it difficult, on the other hand, to enjoy staying inside the house on rainy weekends. It was not familiar and comfortable to him.

"How often do you get out and have fun? How much time each

week do you take for leisure activities?" People can have interests but not take the time to enjoy them. You need to determine if the way the person structures his or her leisure time is compatible with yours. Don't just go by how he or she behaves on dates, since dates are not a true indicator of day-to-day routine and lifestyle.

To find out more about a person's way of recharging, you can ask, "**What do you do when you want to relax?** Where do you go?" Someone who likes to be alone to relax will not want to be pestered by a partner who wants to do things together, and someone who likes to relax talking to their partner will not want to be ignored or abandoned by the other's withdrawal. If your relaxation style is similar, however, your relationship will be that much more satisfying.

A similar direction of inquiry is, "**What kinds of vacations do you like to take?**" To get a comprehensive feel for this topic, it can be helpful to find out what a person did for vacations as a child. Did they go places or not? Were they happy times or not? What did they enjoy about the vacations? These questions give a sense of where a person is coming from and why they have certain current preferences. To know about their present desires, you can ask about what kinds of vacations they would like to take now. Do they have places they find especially conducive to relaxing? Do they like to be active or quiet on vacations? Do they like to be with other people or off secluded when they have time away? Do they like to travel or stay in one place? Answers to these questions bring out much more than preferences for vacations. They will show the person's energy, sociability, and enthusiasm for life. As to the relationship, you can ask, "**What would you like to do with your partner on a vacation?** What would you like your partner to want to do on a vacation?" Because leisure energy is so important, this becomes an important compatibility variable.

Learning about a person's interests and ways of having fun can be fascinating conversation. Many people enjoy talking at length about them. These conversations also bring to light one of the central needs of a relationship: play and leisure. They are essential to a satisfying relationship.

There are questions you can ask to find out about another important element: friendship. You might ask questions such as, **"What are your friendships like and what do you do with your friends?"** Knowing about a person's patterns of friendships will let you know how you might get along as friends and what he or she might expect from you. Some of the practical realities of friendship you might want to look for could include: Would this person be expecting you to go out to dinner with other couples often or would he or she feel awkward around your friends? Is he or she comfortable with your having friends of the opposite sex or would he/she get jealous? If you know his or her friends, do you like them or not? Could you enjoy spending a great deal of time with them?

Since a friendship often involves a Child to Child relationship, you can get some clues about a potential partner's friendship style by asking questions about childhood friendships. **"What were your friendships like when you were growing up?** Did you have many friends or just a few? What are some of your best memories from childhood about friends? What are some of your most painful or frustrating memories? Did kids at school tend to approach you or did you approach them? Or did friendships just happen?" As a couple, you will need to be friends with each other as well as to have friendships you share and have independently. It is useful to know what to expect in this important aspect of life.

Another facet related to the Child ego state has to do with how a person handles tough times, which will surely occur in a relationship. A good question for this is, **"What's the feeling you most often experience when things go wrong and what do you do at those moments?"** If your potential partner withdraws, would you be comfortable with that? If the response is a quick temper or a flurry of activity to change and improve things, how would you like that? The other side of the coin is, **"What do you want from others when things go wrong?"** This shows the expectations your partner will have, and you need to consider how you might respond to these expectations.

Getting to know about the person's Child does not have to be limited to conversations. Watching how they are with others, noticing how they handle surprises, being aware of how they pace themselves, all bring out important features of their inner Child.

One interesting way to learn more about a person is to look at photographs of them. A childhood family photo album works especially well for this purpose. When you look at the pictures, notice the expressions on the person's face. Do they look happy? Do they look involved with the other people in the pictures? What are they doing that can give a clue about how the person is now?

Each person's Child has different ways of reacting to situations and of interacting with others. Because the Child is such a strong determinant of behavior, especially in a love relationship, the more you can share about this aspect of yourselves, the better you both will be able to make a wise decision.

Summary: Interviewing the Inner Child

"What do you like to do for fun?"

"What did you do for fun when you were little?"

"How often do you get out and have fun?

'What do you do when you want to relax?"

"What kinds of vacations do you like to take?"

"What would you like to do with your partner on a vacation?"

"What are your friendships like and what do you do with your friends?"

"What were your friendships like when you were growing up?"

"What's the feeling you most often experience when things go wrong and what do you do at those moments?"

"What do you want from others when things go wrong?"

Are You The One For Me?

Interviewing the Inner Parent

Sometimes what parents have said is remembered as if it were said today, maybe even in the voice that was used. Often people talk like one of their parents, using the same words and tone of voice when relating to a loved one. Larry found himself calling his girlfriend "honey pie," a nickname his father used for his mother.

In addition to what is learned from parents, everyone also learns many important values and beliefs from other significant people in their lives who acted as surrogate parents. Relatives, teachers, family friends, neighbors, baby-sitters, and older siblings can have an enormous impact on a person's attitudes toward love, dating, and marriage.

For example, as a child Frank always looked up to his older brother. His father died in a car accident soon after Frank's birth. Frank thought his brother was the epitome of what a man should be like. Although he never voiced this to anyone, he privately believed that whatever his brother did or said was what he wanted to emulate when he grew up. Frank remembered his brother would sometimes sit with him and talk to him about girls. "Always treat a girl the way you would like her to treat you." This phrase stuck with Frank. When he grew up, he followed his brother's advice. He was honest, thoughtful, and kind whenever he met someone he wanted to date. He was able to use the healthy attitudes he got from his brother effectively as an adult.

People raised by aging grandparents often have something in common. They frequently act especially well behaved as children so as not to burden or disappoint their grandparents. When they grow up, they may be very mature and responsible but have trouble letting themselves have fun. They may still be trying hard to please a lover just as they did with their grandparents. And they may also be hoping to find a partner who is as patient and generous as their grandparents were.

An easy way to get to know about a person's Parent ego state is to watch them around children. They will likely treat your inner Child as they treat children. Since everyone acts like a child at times, you will too, and it's good to know in advance whether or not you'll get good treatment.

There are a number of other things you can look for and questions you can ask that will help you know in advance about the other person's inner Parent.

The most basic question is *"What were your parents like when you were growing up?"* Were they happy, hard-working, tender, available, reasonable, organized? Were they critical, controlling, overnurturing, wishy-washy? Positive attributes of the parents will enhance a relationship when copied; negative aspects will undermine it unless they are deliberately discarded.

Everybody changes with time, even parents. Find out about any significant changes in the person's relationship with his or her parents by asking, *"What are your parents like today,* and how do you get along with them? Do you like them? Are you close to them?"

Another way to get to know about the person's Parent ego state is to pick any topic and ask, *"What were your parents' opinions about marriage (or money, education, friendship, children, sex, food, etc.)?"* For example, when you're going out for ice cream, you might ask what your partner's parents' attitudes were about food and eating. Did they make a big deal about nutrition? Did they make snide remarks about people who ate slowly or gobbled their food? Was there pleasant conversation at the dinner table in your family? Was the woman expected to be the only cook in the family? This information will give you some clues about the external conditioning your partner grew up with.

However, just as important as the role model the parents provide is the person's response to his or her parents and environment. What did he or she think about their opinions? *"How did their opinions influence you then and now?"* Did you agree with parental expectations? Do you believe that these parental patterns should be continued in perpetuity or have you decided to act in other ways?"

Another set of questions to find out more about your partner's parents is to ask "**What advice would your parents give you about dating (or marriage, your career, raising children, arguments, borrowing money, etc.)?**" Phyllis's father was from the old school. He often criticized women and said they were stupid and shouldn't try to do things they couldn't do. Phyllis' mother, much to the consternation of her father, would tell Phyllis that women should be active in the community, involved in women's rights, and doing things to better themselves and others. Phyllis felt stuck. If she tried to please her father, she would have to stay home, in the shadow of some man, waiting anxiously for him to come home to pat her on the head for her cooking and housework. If she wanted to please her mother, she would have to be active, productive, and effective in the real world. The question then becomes, which parental influences will prevail and how will that influence a relationship? The easiest way to discuss this is to ask the person "**Do you tend to favor or follow one parent's advice or do you prefer to follow your own direction?**"

Again, it is important to know if the parents' advice was useful and followed or if it seemed off target and was resisted or ignored. As you listen to the advice, check out whether or not your own parents would agree with your potential partner's parents. If so, your compatibility factor is higher. If not, this could be an area of conflict or at least divided loyalties for you later in your relationship.

Interesting clues to the relationship's future can be spotted early by asking yourselves, "**How would your parents get along with your partner's parents?** How would your mother get along with my father? and How would your father get along with my mother?" If you end up living together, your Parent ego states will also be living together. Those aspects of life in which your parents could get along are areas in which you are likely to be compatible when you're in your Parent ego states. Those areas in which your parents would not get along will probably become tension areas.

For example, if both your parents and his or her parents would agree on the importance of education, then you would likely support each other's efforts to get additional education as you get older. You'd both probably find it easy to make some sacrifices to make sure your children get a good education. But if his or her parents thought education was a waste of time and that a person ought to start at the bottom and work up, then when you live together you might have some major struggles regarding the importance of education for yourselves or your children.

Another question that can give insight into people's probable behavior is "*How did your parents spend their time?* Were they always on the go? Were they involved in their child's life or were they off in their own world? Did they take time to enjoy the family or were they always working, either at the office or in the house or yard?" The modeling a person saw regarding time structuring can have an enduring influence on his or her adult behavior. For example, Craig's parents took time to help him with his homework and go to his baseball games. They included him in family discussions and were open to his opinions, although they reserved the right to the final word. They paid attention to his needs but were not overly permissive or indulgent. Consequently, Craig developed a Parent ego state that included these attributes. When he met Jeannette, he treated her in the same way. He talked with her and listened to her opinions. He took time to enjoy their relationship and made sure he was available to her when she had an important event to go to. He knew her world was as important as his.

Paul, on the other hand, had parents who were always busy. They were either in the garden or the house, cleaning or repairing, from sunup to sundown. His father was very impatient and would get mad if Paul didn't do his chores perfectly. Paul decided then that he had to be busy just like his parents. When he grew up and started to date, he would always be critical of any woman whose apartment or house wasn't spotless. Instead of going out for brunch, he would offer to fix the closet door that was sticking. He was great to have around when something needed to be done, but on a date he could only talk about projects he was working on and what else needed to be done.

"*What was your parents' social life like?* Were they sociable and active or were they reclusive and isolated? Did they have friends over often or not?" Parents' attitudes toward friends will influence a person's love relationship. If someone grows up with parents who entertained frequently, he or she will likely feel competent socializing as an adult. If their parents didn't have friends, they may not know the rules of etiquette for guests and feel awkward having someone drop by or over for a party. Lorraine remembers that her parents "kept our house like a pigsty. I hated it. I would never bring friends over because I didn't want them to see how dirty my house was. Even to this day, I hate to have people stop by unannounced. I'm afraid they'll see the house when it's not cleaned up."

"*How did your parents get along?*" If they got along well, the person will likely have developed skills that he or she can use to create a stable relationship in his or her own life. If his or her parents did not get along well, that may have left a scar. It does not mean, however, that the person is destined to replay the parents' problems. It means that the person had to overcome this programming. So the follow-up question is "*What would you like in your relationship that might be different from your parents' relationship?*"

The areas of conflict or dissatisfaction in parents' relationship will often have a strong impact on the children. "*What were your parents unable to resolve in their relationship?* and "*What was their hang-up as a couple?*" are good questions that will reveal what has helped mold a person's dreams and personality.

A similar set of questions is "*What did your parents disagree on?* Did they fight over money, politics, the kids, sex, free time, chores? "*How did they handle differences of opinion?*" Did they yell and scream, talk sarcastically, withdraw and declare a cold war, or work things out peaceably? Because arguments are such a real part of any relationship, it's useful to know about both the form and content of handling conflicts a prospective mate grew up with.

There are many other specific issues that you can ask about and watch for that can give you clues about what to expect in a relationship. For example, you can watch how people treat others when they are sick. Are they tender or indifferent, available or absent? This will give you a clue as to the treatment you can expect when you are sick. It also shows the treatment they will expect from you when they are sick.

The most important questions about parents you can ask are more global and open-ended: "*Have parental influences and childhood experiences been useful or detrimental to you in previous love relationships? How and when might those parental messages surface again?*"

Using this kind of information exchange, you can get a good idea of what your relationship might be like if you pursue it. Keep in mind that it is important to share similar information with your potential partner so he or she can also have a realistic understanding of you and how you might act in a relationship.

Summary: Interviewing the Inner Parent

"What were your parents like when you were growing up?"

"What are your parents like today? How do you get along with them?"

"What were your parents' opinions about marriage, money, education, friendship, children, sex, food?"

"How did their opinions influence you, then and now?"

"What advice would your parents give you about dating (or marriage, your career, raising children, arguments, borrowing money, etc.)?"

"Do you tend to favor or follow one parent's advice or do you prefer to follow your own direction?"

"How would your parents get along with your partner's parents?"

"How did your parents spend their time?"

"What was your parents' social life like?"

"How did your parents get along?"

"What would you like in your relationship that might be different from your parents' relationship?"

"What were your parents unable to resolve in their relationship? What was their hang-up as a couple?"

"What did your parents disagree on? How did your parents handle differences of opinion?"

"Have parental influences and childhood experiences been useful or detrimental to you in previous love relationships? How and when might those parental messages surface again?"

Interviewing the Inner Adult

The Adult ego state is like a muscle; the more it is used, the stronger it gets. The Adult ego state needs to be well developed in anyone you date. If it is, you can have intelligent conversations and share information. A person with a strong Adult can hold down a good job and is often interested in improving his or her career skills. She or he is able to handle day-to-day tasks efficiently, such as paying bills, keeping the car in good condition, structuring weekend time, and so on.

Equally important, someone with a strong Adult is able to solve problems with you in a rational fashion. He or she is able to recognize feelings as valid concerns, but not let them have the ultimate say. This does not mean that people with strong Adult ego states act like robots and accept only logic as the sole criterion for deciding. Rather they will have the necessary skills to take care of crises, problems, and day-to-day business in a clear-thinking fashion. They will be able to sort out the "shoulds" they were raised with from the realities of the moment of your relationship.

You can rely on them to handle problems as they arise, without minimizing or exaggerating them. They will also be a good ally to have when things get tough or decisions have to be made quickly.

Questions you can ask to learn more about a person's Adult are: *"What do you like to talk about?"* A simple question, but since a large part of a relationship is spent talking, this can let you know about the kinds of conversations you'd likely get into in the future. When you think about this, think in terms of *social currencies*. Social currencies are the topics of conversation people use to make contact with others. They reflect interests in life, as well as values and priorities in structuring their time.[24] For example, some people's social currency is *food*. Their conversation usually circles back to concerns such as diets, recipes, picnics, restaurants, how clothes fit, children's nutrition, digestion and regularity, etc. Another social currency is *power*. Those interested in power tend to talk about authority and be name droppers. They dress and act so people will recognize their importance. They pay attention to power plays around them and enjoy building power networks at work. Others live by *emotions*, always noticing how people, including themselves, feel. They worry about how others feel and are afraid of hurting other people's feelings. They often ride an emotional roller coaster throughout life—if it's not one feeling, it's another. Others live and breathe *money*. Some people are interested in *sex* and flirtation and always seem to be making sexual jokes or innuendos. There are many social currencies. When you recognize your currencies, you can predict what you will talk about and spend time doing as a couple. Then you need to decide how compatible your currencies are.

If you want to get a little riskier, you can ask, *"What conversations do you tend to avoid?"* The answer to this may require more trust or candor than some other questions. But if you can learn about this, you will be able to determine early on if you will find certain topics of conversation a problem. Some people get tense talking about money, others about sex. Some avoid talking about their past or their future. Others hate to talk about anything that would lead to conflict. By avoiding a topic, couples usually end up fighting about it later, so growing couples need to be willing to learn to talk about anything.

"*How have you changed over the years?* How do you explain your changes?" It's interesting to find out about how someone sees themselves changing over the years and to what they attribute their changes. This can show you if they see themselves evolving or wandering, making things happen or being controlled by others. This can also give important insight to the direction the person is headed in the future and how easy or difficult it would be to accompany them on their journey ahead.

"*What are the personal and professional successes you're most proud of?* What have been some of the challenges you've overcome and succeeded at? What are some problems you've encountered while achieving your successes?" Most people enjoy talking about their strengths as long as it doesn't sound like bragging. Ask them about this; you may find the person is quite remarkable in some ways that aren't easily noticed at first.

You can take this line of questioning further by asking, "*What aspects of a relationship are you good at and which ones are difficult for you?*" People know what they're good at. When invited, they will often give a good assessment of themselves. The trick is to listen carefully and not gloss over statements you don't understand. It's better to clarify these issues now than to find out later.

"*What are some of your shortcomings that you would want to work on in a relationship?*" Is there anything you don't like about yourself that you would like to change? Do you have any sense of what you would need to do to make that change? These questions may need to be saved until after you both trust each other. Few people like to talk about their deep heartfelt frustrations when first meeting someone. Yet most people have an awareness of some of their shortcomings. Trying to hide them can drain energy and talking about them can be both interesting and a relief. In fact, being candid about topics such as this can open new frontiers in the relationship.

"*Describe your ideal roommate. Which traits might you enjoy and which traits would irritate you the most?*" It's romantic and useful to talk about what you both are looking for in a partner. This is usually fairly easy. It's also important to discuss what you don't want. You might ask, "How do you feel about: snoring, dirty dishes, nail biting, wearing rollers, talking on the phone, paying bills, chewing gum, cautious driving, loud music, eating in front of TV?" People frequently know what they don't want, so you might as well ask them about it. That way you will know if you fit their "job description" as well as if they fit yours.

"*What are your plans for the future?* In what ways have you started working on them?" It is fun to dream about the future, but the sign of maturity is someone who does something about it. Someone who has some sense of a goal will tend to have a greater investment in building a lasting relationship. They will want to use their time well and not waste it. If the person has some long-range goals that you find interesting, then your compatibility potential increases.

"*How do you like to make decisions?*" Again, each person has their own style of decision making. The way a person makes decisions will have a profound effect on the direction of your relationship. If they make impulsive decisions, will that be too abrupt for you? If they spend long hours pondering, will you find their process too tedious and cautious? If they always look to someone else for advice, can you have confidence in them?

Also find out about how they like to handle things as a couple. "*How do you usually make decisions when someone else is involved?*" You want to find out if the person will be interested in sharing decisions with you? Will the potential partner look to you to decide things? Or will the person expect to make all the decisions, or avoid them entirely, hoping things will somehow work themselves out by magic?

"*How do you solve problems?*" Does the person you are interviewing sound confident about handling things or exaggerate or discount personal responsibilities? Is the person willing to work things out with a partner or does he or she believe that "If you want something done right, you have to do it yourself?" What would be expected from you if you were solving problems as a couple? If you don't agree, how would you handle it? Each person has their own style of problem solving, and none is inherently better or worse than another. But you need to determine if your potential partner's style is one you could live with.

In addition to general questions there are also numerous nitty-gritty issues that are helpful to determine early. For example, "*What are your attitudes toward household chores?* Which ones are you willing to do or get done and which ones would you expect a partner to do?" Many, many people argue over these kinds of issues. Who's supposed to pick up the clothes he leaves on the floor? Who's supposed to pay bills? Who's going to do the washing and ironing? Years ago these answers were assumed without question. But today you will probably need to know if your potential partner has traditional assumptions, a new approach, or a blend of the two.

Another very important specific question is "*What are your attitudes and style of handling money?*" This is often a touchy question. It must be addressed, since one of the biggest problems in many marriages has to do with money management. If people have significantly different styles of handling money, they can spend many frustrating hours arguing. One does not necessarily learn about another person's attitudes by watching how they spend money on a date. In fact that can be very misleading. A person who acts very generous on a date may in fact be very stringent with their money later on.

"*Do you feel comfortable talking about sex?*" This is obviously not usually an appropriate question on the first date. For most, it is far too personal. But it is useful to find out as soon as possible rather than when you're so emotionally involved you can't collect data rationally. Most couples go through some periods of sexual frustration in a relationship. If they can't talk about it, how can they work it out? The problem with this question may be that you may have some reservations about talking about sex and, therefore, find this difficult to ask someone you don't know well. If that's the case, wait until later to find out.

Summary: Interviewing the Inner Adult

"What do you like to talk about?"

"What conversations do you tend to avoid?"

"How have you changed over the years?"

"What are your personal and professional successes you're most proud of?"

"What aspects of a relationship are you good at and which ones are difficult for you?"

"What are some of your shortcomings that you would want to work on in a relationship?"

"Describe your ideal roommate. Which traits might you enjoy and which traits would irritate you the most?"

"What are your plans for the future?"

"How do you like to make decisions?"

"How do you usually make decisions when someone else is involved?"

"How do you solve problems?"

"What are your attitudes toward household chores?"

"What are your attitudes and style of handling money?"

"Do you feel comfortable talking about sex?"

Are You The One For Me?

Exercise: What Questions Do You Want Answered?

There may be some questions not included in the above interview that are important, maybe even crucial, to you. Take a moment and think about what these might be. Jot them down so you will remember them easily.

_____

_____

_____

_____

_____

_____

_____

_____

_____

_____

_____

_____

_____

_____

A Word to the Wise

The questions and points of interest mentioned in the interview are not meant to imply that people should pick partners using a cold and calculated approach. Try to maintain a playful atmosphere where both people are willing to interview the other. In fact, you could even be deliberate about setting up the interview; suggest it as a novel way to spend the evening! If the other person interviews you or if you interview yourself, you'll probably find out some new and interesting facets to your personality.

The more you know about the other person in advance, the wiser your decision will be. Then if your relationship turns to love, it will be based on a foundation of knowledge, not just hopes and fantasies.

Chapter 6

ɯɔɔ

ROMANCE AND THE BEGINNING OF LOVE

*"I didn't know anyone could be so perfect.
He's my ideal of everything a man could be.
For years I've been searching for him.
Sometimes it's felt like I was chasing a
rainbow. But finally I've found him!"*

*"When I met her, I felt as if the world was
giving way under my feet. It was a strong
sensation, like falling into a cloud. It wasn't
scary; it was just different from anything I
ever experienced before and the odd thing
about it was that I didn't care."*

*"He loves me, he loves me not . . .
Sometimes I'm sure he does, sometimes I'm
not. Sometimes I feel like I'm in heaven, other
times in hell. I begin to wonder, Is this what
romance is all about?"*

Falling in love is one of the most special events in a person's life. Everyone wants to be in love, and when it happens, life comes alive. You are suddenly filled with energy, enthusiasm, and desire, as everything seems to click. There's a special chemistry at work. Time is too short when lovers are together and too long when they're apart.

The early moments of love and romance are often filled with exciting adventures and intense passion. Candlelight dinners, long drives, quiet talks, and tender moments are frequent activities in this phase. So are spontaneous weekends camping or traveling, running in the park or scuba diving, having midnight snowball fights or star gazing.

During this time, many couples believe they have found what they've been waiting for—their dream of the perfect partner. They tend to see each other romantically, rather than as they really are.

This chapter is about romance and the romantic feelings and thoughts people have when they are caught up in the early magic of falling in love. You will learn about love at first sight and how love affects the brain and the body, as well as the agony and the ecstacy that people in love experience. It also examines the shared dream that ensues during this romantic period, how people idealize each other and try to live up to those ideals themselves. Also considered are the challenges couples in love need to achieve to ensure a solid foundation for their future relationship.

The Patterns of Romance

People often confuse the word *romance* with the word *love.* Clichés and slogans such as "falling in love" make the confusion worse. "Falling in love" is only the first phase of romance. Romance includes sentimental feelings, passionate behavior, and the idealization of the partner. Sometimes romance leads to love, sometimes it leads to tragedy, sometimes it leads to indifference and separation.

During the Romance stage of a relationship, three things usually happen: falling in love, the idealization of the loved one, and sharing and blending of life dreams. Dreams and high hopes of living "happily ever after" are ignited and become driving forces in the relationship. Usually both persons idealize their new love in order to create and sustain their dreams. Both try to show their best side and believe they have something special to give and will also receive something special in return. As a couple, they develop shared dreams and make promises to each other about these dreams. They also try to make their personal dreams fit together with their partner's dreams so that they can be the ideal couple. As these processes lay much of the groundwork for the couple's future life together, each is worth examining more closely.

Falling in Love

When couples fall in love they experience glorious and curious emotional changes. Many feel spellbound, as if they've known their partner forever and have met in a previous lifetime. For some, the feeling is one of being "transported to another world" where nothing is more important than being with the loved one. Lovers commonly express this by saying, "I knew she was the one I wanted to marry when I first saw her," or "We were meant for each other. It was destiny." For many, other cares and woes fade into the background. During this initial period, some lovers may experience what has been called "a temporary state of imbecility" because it is so often a manic-depressive experience, feeling high when things are going well with the loved one, feeling depressed when things are not going well.[25] People who observe the relationship may call it "infatuation" but those involved call it "love."

Definitions make communication clearer. But when it comes to defining "love," definitions are inadequate. One person may say, "Love is commitment." Another may say, "Love means taking care of each other." Still others may say, "Love is sacrificing your own needs for the well-being of the other person." Then there are people who define love in terms of beauty, pride, or power. No definition of love can encompass the totality of people's experience when falling in love. Love is too mysterious and multifaceted. Furthermore, each person has a unique mind-set of love and of what loving means.

Exercise: What Love Means to You

Love means different things to different people. You're looking for someone who thinks of love as you do. Take a few moments to think about it:

What is your definition of love?

_____

_____

_____

_____

What are your opinions about "falling in love"?

_____

_____

_____

_____

Do you tend to fall in love, move into it slowly, stumble into it, pass it by, or walk away from it?

_____

_____

_____

Have you developed any mind-sets about yourself and falling in love? If so, what are they?

_____

_____

_____

Preconditions for Falling In Love

However love is defined, there is interesting research that sheds new light on the preconditions for falling in love. First, people must have been raised in a culture or family that believes in the concept and teaches it to young people. In the United States, for example, the continuous flood of romantic adventures, especially on TV and in other mass media, teaches people about the notion of "falling in love"—and teaches them to expect to experience it. This creates a mind-set that makes falling in love preferable to almost any other state of being. It is not surprising that by the time children reach adolescence they not only *want* to fall in love but they are *expected* to do so by peers and culture.[26]

The second precondition is that the more people *think* about love with positive expectations, the more likely they are to experience it. Believing that "love at first sight" can occur may be enough to create the positive expectation that it will happen. In contrast, people who don't think about love or have strong doubts about it seldom find their right partner.[27]

Love at First Sight

Falling in love is often a sudden experience of love at first sight. Those who have experienced it tend to believe in it; those who have not, do not. One study reported that more than 50 percent of the adults queried reported falling in love at first sight at least once in their life.[28]

Paul reported, "I always knew it would happen to me. The day I saw her, I knew immediately that she was the one I had been waiting for. After meeting her, we went for a long walk and we talked and talked. I was totally enchanted by her. I knew then that my waiting had ended and that dreams do come true." His partner Laura commented, "I thought love at first sight only happened in movies or to other people because I always considered myself somewhat of a practical person. But when I saw him, I changed my mind. I know now that it really happens to people because it happened to me!"

Sometimes love at first sight doesn't work out. Tom recalled with sadness, "I really thought she was the one. She seemed to fit everything I wanted. When I first met her, she was warm, beautiful, and considerate. But later she turned out to be just the opposite. After two years, we broke up. I understand now it was a mistake to let myself get so caught up in the enchantment of the first evening together and the fantasy of how our future life could be." Anyone can fall in love, but it doesn't guarantee future success in the relationship. So don't forget to interview your partner before giving your heart away. It may save you a lot of pain later. The exercise on the right-hand page can help you clarify your thoughts about love at first sight.

I Can't Get You Out of My Mind!

For many couples, their romance becomes so intense that they find themselves constantly thinking about each other. Even a momentary absence from the other person whets their emotional appetite for closeness.

Obsessive concentration on the loved one is a characteristic of the early phase of romance. This continual interest in the partner is natural and adds excitement to the relationship. Lucy reported, "I go to bed thinking about what we did together during the day. Then I dream about him and wake up wanting to be with him all over again."

Exercise: Have You Ever Fallen in Love at First Sight?

Take a few moments to think about the loves in your past:

Have you ever experienced love at first sight? If so, what did you feel and think in those moments?

_____

_____

_____

_____

Was your experience positive and worthwhile, or confusing and misleading?

_____

_____

_____

_____

As you look back now, what did you learn from the experience? Would you want to fall in love again? Would you use a different approach?

_____

_____

_____

_____

When they're apart, it is fairly common for people caught in the upswell of romance to wait anxiously for the doorbell or phone to ring and have it be their loved one. Throughout the day and night, little events that happen remind them of each other. A song on the radio, a restaurant, a sunset, or a scene in a movie may spark memories of their time together and their desire to be together again.

People like this also spend hours discussing their lover with close friends or family. Their enthusiasm may be so strong that they forget that friends can get bored listening to their stories. This kind of emotional immersion in their loved one can become so intense that other responsibilities are ignored. Carlos explained, "I find it hard to concentrate on my work and it's just piled up. I tell myself I should get to work, but instead I find myself daydreaming about being together. The other day, I was at a meeting and someone asked me a question. I didn't even hear the question. I didn't know what was going on until other people started to laugh."

Love's Chemistry

Love has been shown to affect not only people's emotions but also their brain chemistry. One study concluded that once the emotional state is defined as love, there is an increase in the brain chemical phenylethylamine that maintains the emotional high. Interestingly, this is the same chemical compound found in chocolate, the most popular gift on Valentine's Day.[29]

Being in love not only affects people's brain chemistry, it can also affect their eating habits. Loss of appetite is for many people one of the first signs of being in love. As one woman reported, "It's too bad you can't stay in the early stages of love forever. If I could, I'd never have to go on a diet again."

Love has other physical side effects. Imagine for a moment that you see your lover approaching you at a party or down a sidewalk. How might you feel? Some people experience physiological reactions such as sweaty hands, butterflies in the stomach, dilation of the pupils, rapid heart beat, and so on.

On the other hand, imagine how it would be for couples who have been together five, ten, or twenty years if every time they saw each other they experienced these same physiological reactions. These reactions tend to occur only in the early stages of

romance or when the partners haven't seen each other for a while.
As couples get to know and love each other, they relax and feel
more comfortable. Disconcerting physiological reactions tend to
fade.

The Agony and Ecstasy of Love

After falling in love, many couples go through intense ups and
downs, often called "the agony and ecstasy of love." Heaven may
be experienced in moments of physical intimacy or when an
unexpected and pleasant event occurs, like having your lover show
up an hour earlier than expected or receiving a poem written just
for you. Hell may be experienced when a lover acts interested in
someone else or is late for a date or preoccupied with work. Even
when the relationship is going well, a minor comment or event
can move some lovers from joy to tears, and hearing the words "I
love you" often reverses the process.

Family or friends may add to the agony or ecstasy. If they
approve of the relationship, the excitement of being together is
increased. If they disapprove, it may create tension and
unhappiness.

Exercise: What's Happened to You?

Think of a time you "fell in love." What happened to you
physically? How did you behave and how was it different from your
usual behavior?

_____

_____

_____

_____

_____

Is there any pattern in how you behave in a new relationship? Do you tend to fall head over heels all at once, or do you tend to proceed at a calm and steady pace? Once in a relationship do you go through a series of emotional highs and lows or do you experience some other pattern? Briefly describe your pattern:

_____

_____

_____

_____

_____

_____

Is this pattern comfortable for you or do you want to change it in any way? If so, how?

_____

_____

_____

_____

_____

What simple resolution or agreement with yourself might you make and keep in mind so your next romance will go more the way you want it to?

_____

_____

_____

_____

_____

_____

Idealizing the Loved One

There is a strong tendency for lovers to idealize each other as "the perfect mate." When in love, they tend to see not only what is but also what could be. With their dreams aflame, each wants to see the other in the best of all possible lights, concentrating on certain positive traits and ignoring negative ones. They see beneath the surface to positive qualities and strengths that exist in seedling form in the partner and imagine these qualities will grow with caring and encouragement.

Idealizing a loved one is natural and makes the moments of early love sweet. The idealized partner's shortcomings are minimized with comments such as, "It's not that important, I can live with it," or "It doesn't really matter. Our love is strong enough to overcome anything."

This belief that love can conquer all has its roots in "the Hollywood Syndrome." The silver screen has given us images of couples who end up in each other's arms, regardless of the obstacles. We all know life isn't always so generous, but we get subliminally conditioned to hope our love lives will be Hollywood-like. Consequently, we are willing (and sometimes even eager) to live with some drama and intrigue to continue the romantic dream.

People who are in love with being in love are not the only ones who ignore their partner's shortcomings. A new lover may notice that his partner doesn't have many friends, but fantasizes that this will change after they've been together a while and she gets to know his friends better. Or she may notice that he doesn't seem to worry too much about how he spends money, but she figures this will change once they start to work for their own home or have kids.

Although some people are willing to call attention to a partner's shortcomings, others are not. They imagine that if they get uptight and talk to a partner about how they feel, it might mean the end of the romance, which is a price they are not willing to pay. Instead they compromise and hope that love will bring out the best at some later time.

Idealizing a partner may appear foolish to outsiders. Have you ever tried to talk someone out of getting married when they were in the Romance stage? It's not likely to work. While outsiders may be able to see the obvious, the person in love may be so enraptured with their partner or with getting married that they do not see their partner as he or she really is.

For example, her parents may recognize that he is rigid and volatile and tell her that they don't think he's the right man for her. But because she loves him so much, she doesn't want to hear this. Or his best friend may mention something about how she seems to have moods and attitudes that are too different from his, but he may be enjoying the contrast. Or in spite of her best friend's warnings that he will never get a divorce, she may choose to believe that he will leave his wife as soon as she's ready to move in with him. People in love see their partner in the best light and defend their image from outside criticism and attack as well as from their own objective evaluation.

Compensatory Fantasies

Even when people in love do acknowledge their partner's shortcomings, there is a tendency for them to imagine their love will compensate for their partner's inadequacies. "He's too serious, but once we are together, I'll help him learn to have fun." "She's unsure of herself but with my support she'll feel more confident."

People also imagine that their partner will bring out their own latent strengths. "She was so sociable, I figured that I'd learn from her how to relax more around other people." "I knew I wasn't good at maintaining the car and figured he would be able to do this for us."

Many people carry with them emotional hungers left over from their earliest relationships with their parents and siblings. The pain of being left alone too much, the injustice of emotional or physical abuse, the pressure of not being able to live up to others' expectations, the fears of being criticized or ridiculed, can all leave scars.

As adults, people with these scars look for partners who will help them heal these old wounds. Someone raised with constant battling in the home is likely to look for a partner who will not be argumentative. Someone raised in a strict regime may search for a partner who is relaxed and casual. A man whose mother was critical may look for a wife who will be continually nurturing and reassuring. He may act like a needy little kid in order to get her to act loving. Or a woman whose parents were always telling her what to do and how to do it, may look for a man who respects her very strong need for independence and will not make critical judgments of her as her parents often did.

Just as people hunger to get their psychological needs met by their partner, they also may want to somehow fill up their partner's emotional reservoir if it is low. They often hope to give their partner the wonderful love they imagine he or she never got before. Margaret saw her boyfriend as a man who had never really had a woman who loved him well. "I took it on as a crusade to make up for this. I helped him set up a small business so he could finally have a chance to become stable. I bought him some new clothes and a car so he could feel better about himself. I spent hours trying to do things for him so that he'd feel loved." In fact, Margaret had a need to rescue men as she had been unable to rescue her severely depressed father in childhood. The problem was her boyfriend didn't want someone to act like a mother to him all the time. He felt smothered by her attention and continual interference in his life.

Living Up to an Ideal

Some people, in an attempt to woo their partner, show only their best sides and withhold other parts of themselves. They believe that who they really are is either "not enough" or "too much" so they try to live up to what they think their partner wants or expects.

She may not let him know about her periodic disinterest in her job because she sees him being so dedicated to his work. Or he may not talk about his fear of going back to school because he doesn't want her to know he sometimes feels stupid. He may "forget" to mention the realities of his problems with his kids, hoping that they will get better by the time they live together. She may decide not to say anything about the way he leaves his clothes around the house because she doesn't want him to think she's a nag. Yet later when they're married, the opinions she held back may become more important when his kids come to visit or when she gets tired of picking up after him. They may both find their inevitable conflict surprising because each seemed so understanding before.

Exercise: Truth or Consequences

Think of an important relationship you've been in. Did you risk being yourself or did you withhold parts of yourself? If you held back parts of yourself, what were they?

_____

_____

_____

_____

What were your reasons for withholding those aspects of yourself?

_____

_____

_____

_____

What were the consequences of censoring yourself in those ways?

_____

_____

_____

_____

Were your reasons based on some preexisting mind-set or a result of your partner's behavior?

_____

_____

_____

_____

Would you do this again or have you decided to show more of who you are?

_____

_____

_____

_____

Too often in the Romance stage, people show censored and edited versions of themselves to their partners. Instead of letting themselves be fully known, some people only show the positive highlights of themselves. Unfortunately, their partner doesn't get the full picture of who they are, only the positive excerpts.

The problem in trying to live up to a partner's dream is that there is a strong tendency to play roles that don't fit well enough to live in. Partners who try to live up to an ideal often become tense and dissatisfied, but not really know how to give up their act. They may think, "This isn't really me, but if I am myself, he [or she] won't love me." Being imprisoned in a false image and being afraid to break free can become a way of life that may temporarily delay or avoid conflict, yet inevitably this leads to unhappiness later. The charade needs to end if a couple wants to enjoy life and have a relationship that lasts.

Shared Dreams

Couples in love want their relationship to last forever. They want to love and be loved and to be able to trust that their love will continue. The dream of getting married and living happily ever after is one many people have. Each person also has his or her unique mosaic of dreams about how a relationship should be. Furthermore, each person hopes to find a partner with similar dreams.

On the first Sunday Karen and Carl spent together, he took her to the beach where they climbed on the rocks looking for starfish. This was something Carl had always loved to do on his own. When he found out that Karen also enjoyed this, he felt he had been given the gift of a lifetime: her dream was similar to his.

Like Karen and Carl, people in love often believe they have found someone who can make their dreams come true. Couples in love often experience a renewed feeling of importance and purpose in their lives. "Now someone really loves me, I don't have to dream alone anymore." Their dreams grow stronger and acquire new meaning. Now what they do matters to someone. Instead of going about life on "automatic pilot," they begin to take charge and take action. This heightened sense of direction gives so much meaning to life that some lovers feel as if they can do anything they set their minds to.

When two people fall in love, one of the pivotal events that also occurs is that they blend many of their individual dreams into a shared dream that they both want. For many couples it is common to want the American dream—one marriage and two of everything else. One couple talked of having two houses (one in the city and another in the country), two kids (a son who plays baseball and a daughter who takes ballet), two cats, two cars, two TV sets, and two jobs to pay all the bills their dream would require.

Shared dreams are like glue to a relationship; they pull the couple together into a united force working for the same goals. When "your dreams" and "my dreams" become "our dreams," a couple feels like they have a target they are shooting for, a destiny worth striving for.

Dreams Become Promises

Dreams easily lead to promises, whether verbalized or not. One common promise is that the romance and love will be given priority over all other relationships and interests in the person's life. This leads to an implied promise of commitment and exclusiveness.

In their exclusiveness, romantic couples spend long hours disclosing intimate information about themselves. They get to know each other better and better and begin to make many more promises to each other. She says, "Promise me you'll never leave me," and he promises to be with her forever. He says, "Promise me you'll never go out with anyone else," and she says she will always be faithful. "Promise that you'll never talk about my most inner secrets," and they both agree. "I promise that I'll bring you roses on our anniversary and I won't go out on Friday nights with my buddies." "I promise to take care of the children and go to your softball games on Sundays." These promises can lay the foundations for future successes or eventual disappointments.

In spite of the fact that some promises may not come true, promises are made as attempts to design a lifestyle that is pleasing to both partners. Often made with the best of intentions, promises fan the flames of romance and this adds excitement to the relationship.

Even if people are sincere about the promises they make to each other, life events and day-to-day routines can relegate their dreams and promises to the back burner where they may be postponed or forgotten. Yet they can be resurrected and brought back to life at any time by a couple who want their relationship to grow.

Exercise: **Making Promises**

Think of an important relationship you had in the past. What promises did your partner make to you?

_____

_____

_____

_____

_____

What promises did you make to your partner?

_____

_____

_____

_____

_____

Did you keep your promises to each other? Which promises were kept and which were not? What effect did that have on your relationship?

_____

_____

_____

_____

_____

Are You The One For Me?

What advice about making promises would you give a good friend who just fell in love?

_____

_____

_____

_____

_____

Will you follow your own advice?

_____

_____

_____

_____

_____

The Challenges of Romance

The philosopher-theologian Martin Buber pointed out that the origin of all conflict in relationships is "that I do not say what I mean, and that I do not do what I say."[30] The advice he would give is obvious. To keep a relationship alive and well, be who you are in word and deed. Say what is true for you and then act accordingly.

Above all, be honest with your partner. Your honesty about yourself and what you want or foresee in the future will set the groundwork for your relationship. If you can accept your partner for who he or she is, your relationship will be likely to develop with less tension and with deeper love. Being honest about who you are is the chance you need to take if you're serious about being and having the right partner.

Furthermore, to avoid feeling discouraged or disappointed later, make promises that are as realistic as possible. This is a challenge for all couples in the Romance stage but the more realistic the promises are, the more they will be able to achieve later.

The challenges of the Romance stage are to eventually give up the excitement of the chase yet maintain intensity and passion, to get to know each other at a deeper and more intimate level, and to solidify realistic commitments to each other. To move to a more mature and lasting love, it is necessary to transform the passionate love of romance into a more companionate love, where each enjoys the other's company and be best friends, with a more realistic knowledge and concern for each other. This is a good time for a couple to decide to live together or to get married and settle in.

Chapter 7

∽ʋↄↄↄↄↄↄↄↄↄↄↄ∽

THE DYNAMICS OF CHANGE

"I could hardly sleep at night I was so excited when we first started living together. Now by the end of the day, I'm so pooped I can hardly keep my eyes open."

"We don't hug and kiss all the time. The need for that kind of intensity has disappeared. But there's time now. We know it won't go away—there's just not the urgency anymore."

"Nine to five, we work. Six to ten, we're together. That's our schedule. Day-in day-out. An hour to get home from work, an hour to prepare and have dinner, and hour to watch the news. The cleaning, the shopping, the washing, the yard—that's for weekends. What happened to our dream?"

"We do all right when we both feel good, but at the first sign of conflict, we seem to pull apart. We want to make our relationship work, but we really don't know how."

All relationships go through changes, so before making your final decision to live together or get married, it's a good idea to look ahead and anticipate the changes your relationship is likely to go through. For example, imagine that your relationship becomes predictable and routine—is that good or bad? If the two of you have conflicts, does it mean you've made a mistake and you're not right for each other? If your differences become entrenched, does it mean you should separate or just make some midcourse adjustments?

This chapter will help you answer these questions by presenting the typical stages or phases many couples go through. These are: the Routine stage, the Conflict stage, the Disillusionment stage, and the Transformation stage. Some couples go through these stages in sequential order. Others seem to skip a stage and go, for example, from Routine to Disillusionment or from Conflict to Transformation. Most couples do not experience a sharp change between one stage and another. Rather, they find their relationship in overlapping stages. Furthermore, one person may be experiencing the relationship in one stage and the partner experience another.

Each stage has value and poses challenges for you as a couple. If you meet those challenges, you may grow in the knowledge that you are right for each other and that your relationship can last for many years, perhaps even a lifetime. If the challenges are not met, the relationship may bog down and lose its vitality. Therefore, knowing what can happen in each stage will help you forecast the future of your relationship. You can gain a more balanced perspective for making your final decision about a partner who is right for you.

The Routine Stage

Romance may burn bright for a while, but as most people realize, the glow eventually fades. The practical necessities of life take over and routines get established. The stage begins almost imperceptibly at times, when each starts to treat the other in predictable ways and expects the other to respond according to established routines. This is the time when couples have the chance to transform the passion and excitement of early love into the predictability and stability of a seasoned love.

Of course it's natural for couples to get into routines—routine ways of doing things and routine ways of treating each other. Couples establish routines in order to bring structure and predictability into their lives. Each gets to know when their partner likes to get up in the morning and go to sleep at night, if he leaves the toothpaste top off or if she leaves the bathroom floor wet after taking a shower. Each gets to know what the other likes to eat and when. Each discovers the other's routines because of their continual contact.

Routines develop in any relationship. Sometimes these routines build a sense of security; other times they lead to conflict or boredom. Coming home from work at a predictable time and sharing news of the day can be a pleasant routine. Coming home from work two or three hours late without notifying one's partner can become a negative routine.

The Value of Routine

Routine provides security and security is necessary for personal and marital health. Everyone needs to feel secure—physically and emotionally—and satisfying routines help fill this need.

Positive routines make life easier; we do them in a way that seems to come naturally and without effort. Positive routines increase the predictability of a relationship. People like to know what to expect from each other so they do not have to worry about being caught by surprise. The habit of kissing goodnight before rolling over to sleep is a good routine for ending the day. The habit of safe driving can make a weekend excursion a relaxed journey.

For a relationship to flourish, partners need to know how their basic physical needs for food, clothing, and shelter will be met. For some couples these basic needs are a continuous and predominant concern. Other couples may worry about them and yet know that somehow they will be able to get by. Still others do not worry at all about physical or financial needs, such as whether they can afford to repair a leaky roof. It is important for couples to know that they can meet their monthly bills, that they have insurance in case of a crisis, and that they have a retirement plan that will be sufficient.

One study of wives of top corporate executives and wives of middle-level managers observed that the wives of executives were more satisfied with their marriages than the midlevel managers' wives. The study concluded that the reason wives of executives were more satisfied was because "they can control the people and events in their lives more easily . . . freedom from financial worries and the ability to pursue one's interests make for fairly happy lives."[31]

Some emotional security is also vital. Emotional security also comes as couples learn that they can count on each other for loving and responsible support. Then they can rely on each other to talk things out when times get tough, to comfort each other when one feels down, and to be willing to compromise personal comfort or opinions for the good of the relationship. Couples feel emotionally secure when they know where they stand and what to expect. For example, in a relationship with traditional values, she trusts that if she has a flat tire, she can phone and he will be there to help. And he trusts that he can phone and, on short notice, she will have dinner ready to entertain his business associates.

When couples can't count on each other, the relationship is in trouble. Worrying about a spouse spending the money irresponsibly, or having affairs, or coming home drunk, or withdrawing and sulking, or being abusive to you or the kids does not contribute to the sense of emotional security.

A sense of emotional security also comes from the familiarity living together can create. Remember the feeling of coming home from a trip to your familiar surroundings? Somehow nothing feels as good as climbing into your own bed with your own pillow and sheets and snuggling up to the one you love. The longer a couple is together, the more familiar their possessions, their habits, and their routines get.

Shared responsibilities are routine behaviors that provide the emotional security that ties a couple together. Shared responsibility may be the household chores or gardening or raising children. While operating as a twosome, couples can gain a sense of camaraderie and teamwork that can bring them closer together.

In a long relationship, people often develop a strong sense of responsibility toward their partner. Having set off on a journey together, they want it to be successful. Sometimes couples become like a loving brother and sister team who could not imagine forcing the other to endure unnecessary hardships. Although they sometimes long for the old excitement of the Romance stage, the routines they've built up can be stabilizing, satisfying, and worth maintaining.

The Challenges of Routine

The Routine stage also poses many challenges. Routines and habits often lead to couples taking each other for granted. Some people think that being taken for granted means that they are being used or unappreciated. But couples who are right for each other often find that being taken for granted can be a very positive experience if based on trust.

People often get distracted and preoccupied and pay attention to whatever seems most immediate or the most stressful instead of paying attention to each other. One or both may begin to think that the routines they have gotten into are not what they imagined their ideal relationship would include. Work, child care, shopping, cooking, cleaning, paying bills—the list of chores that demand routines seems endless.

In the Dating and Romance stages, people are usually on their best behavior. Then as the routines are established, unexpected behaviors and expectations emerge and the relationship begins to change. Barriers are relaxed and more of the real self shows. What was held back in the Romance stage is often expressed in the Routine stage. It is as if the person assumes, "Now that somebody really loves me, I can finally be myself."

Problems arise if the unexpected behaviors and new expectations seem unreasonable and unfair. For example, he may expect her to be sexually uninhibited and enjoy sex daily and she may only expect to have sex on weekends. She may feel pressured by his overenthusiasm and he may feel rejected by her seeming disinterest. They need to find a way to compromise so both are satisfied.

For many couples, new behaviors are viewed as undesirable. The partner has changed and is not acting how he or she did when they first got together. The original attraction that drew them together in the first place may be forgotten. Certainly it *wasn't* the household chores nor the bills that drew them together. It *was* the time they spent with each other—talking and laughing and enjoying, the time they spent creating dreams instead of solving problems.

Day-to-day problems can lead couples to wonder if their old life dreams of a satisfying relationship will ever come true or if there is something wrong with their partner and/or their relationship. Often they focus on what's going wrong with the *product* of their dreams: the kids, the house, the car, the adult toys, and they forget to nurture their relationship. They forget that the *process* of going for their dreams is the more essential challenge. They forget that it is possible to enjoy time together no matter what they're doing.

Routines can last a long time or can be outgrown. If not satisfying, they can also be deliberately changed. Sometimes partners become aware of the need for change and try to make things better by being placating or appeasing by avoiding disagreements and fights. In effect, they are trying to get back the sense of enjoyment and togetherness they once felt in the Romance stage. When couples make these adjustments, they may withhold their resentments and disagreements which need to be dealt with. If these problems are avoided, they may surface later during the Conflict stage.

The Conflict Stage

It would be great if marriage was easy—but sometimes it's not. Everyone knows it isn't. It requires a lot of work and a bit of luck. And anyone who's been married any length of time will tell you that there are times in all marriages when couples experience power struggles and conflict. They're inevitable —but not necessarily bad.

In the Dating and Romance stages, couples may fight occasionally but usually the squabbles get worked out. In the Routine stage, conflicts become a more frequent companion to the relationship. In fact, some routines are carved out by the chisels of arguments. Couples sometimes have to fight to shape their relationship as they want it to be.

A conflict can be a minor disagreement, a collision of values, a contest for power, or a battle. It can be mild competition or an angry fight. It can be physical and/or emotional, with or without words.

Without words, conflict can be like a cold war where sex and affection are withheld and silence maintained. A cold war is usually meant to manipulate, intimidate, or punish, often so that the other person will feel guilty and change. With words, the war may heat up and disagreements can become bitter, sarcastic, and accusatory, wearing away at the foundation of love and trust.

There comes a time when many couples get locked into opposing attitudes and power struggles that seem never to end.

Even when the fighting subsides for a while, the underlying conflict remains. Finding themselves continually fighting or distant and withdrawn, couples feel trapped in the Conflict stage. Even in the best of relationships, there are times when dreams and routines get overshadowed by differences and disagreements. This may be inevitable—but it is not necessarily bad if the couple learns from their conflicts.

In the early moments of the relationship, when passions were high and love intense, dreams were shared and promises were made. Each person counted on the dreams to become realities. Then, in the Routine stage, the dreams faded or the promises weren't kept and one or both parties ended up feeling cheated. Perhaps each got involved in different activities—focusing their attention on children, chores, or crises or on obtaining possessions, prestige, or power instead of on spending time together as a couple. Perhaps each lost sight of the dreams they once shared and their relationship began to become more of a job than a joy.

Broken promises and the sense of injustice they create are often at the core of the Conflict stage. Consequently, feeling a bit desperate, a couple may begin to fight to get back on track with their dreams. If this happens, they can get locked into opposing positions and their problems remain unresolved. Power plays escalate, insults linger, and apologies are delayed or never come. The fighting may subside for periods of time but unless there is a conscious resolution of the issues, the choice of partner may begin to seem to have been the "wrong" one.

Exercise: Past Conflicts and Dreams

As you think about your past dreams, you may be able to understand the evolution of your relationship from romance to routine to conflict.

Think of a past relationship you were once in or one you are in now. Recall some of the dreams you had at the beginning of the relationship. Which ones came true?

_____

_____

_____

_____

_____

Which ones changed in some way?

_____

_____

_____

_____

Which ones did you fight for or give up on?

_____

_____

_____

_____

_____

The Reasons Couples Fight

The major reason couples fight is because the romantic promises weren't kept and their dreams seemed to be put on the back burner or totally ignored. Naturally each begins to feel angry.

Their dreams are too important to give up without a fight!

Once the fights begin, however, there are secondary reasons that keep them going. These reasons are usually interwoven and difficult to separate. Yet they can be unraveled and understood one at a time when couples know what to look for.

Couples usually fight for one or more of the following reasons:

1. To break the routine and spark some excitement

2. To maintain control and stay comfortable

3. To minimize their differences

4. To be understood and appreciated

5. To cope with their partner's moods and actions

6. To be right and not be made wrong

7. To hold on to or break up old loyalties

8. To balance the scales of justice

9. To define, develop, and express a separate identity

10. To find new solutions to old problems

Each reason is important and needs to be considered so that you can discover what, why, and how you deal with conflict.

1. *The Excitement Factor* emerges out of the need to break the routine and spark some newness. Couples fight because they want a change of pace. Routines get to be too much and too old too soon. Routine conversations, evenings, sex, weekends, even routine fights—things can get predictable and busy without being emotionally involving. When rituals become habitual ways of filling in time, done without thought or real

benefit, then they become meaningless. Many people want more than this. They believe that life was meant to be lived, not just endured. Their urge for excitement is high so they stir up the waters of discontent to get something new to occur.

2. ***The Comfort and Control Factor*** occurs because most people like to live in the comfort of their own routines. Their familiar ways of doing things are what they want. Problems can arise when one person wants a change and the other does not want to move from the "Comfort Zone." She had taken care of the children for a long time and now wants to go out and work. This may threaten his comfort. He does not want her to go to work and "neglect her duties" and, furthermore, he doesn't want to talk about it.

   People have a deep-seated urge for freedom and self-determination. This gets ignited when someone else tries to impose unreasonable expectations on them. It is as if they are saying, "What makes you think you can tell me what to do? I'm not going to put up with your nagging any more!"

3. ***The Difference Factor*** results from one or both persons trying to minimize their differences to stay together. Some couples are able to forge a mutually satisfying blend of their differences. They welcome their differences as strengths and as counterbalances for their shortcomings. Other people forget that they choose their partner precisely for some of their different ways of doing things. Instead of enjoying these differences, they fight about them.

   Yet some differences are annoying or intolerable. Annoying differences might include his impatience or her oversensitivity, her nail biting or his carelessness. Intolerable differences are even more problematic. She may find it impossible to tolerate his drinking or coming home late. He may find it hard to live with her chain-smoking. She may not be willing to accept his continual arguing with the kids. He may not accept her continuous complaining. The list of differences is endless.

It is these kinds of intolerable differences that couples often fight about the hardest. For many, there comes a time when enough is enough and even minor differences can no longer be tolerated. That's when warfare can break out.

4. *The Appreciation Factor* is a result of a person's need to be understood and appreciated. In fact one of the most common reasons people get into power struggles is that they feel their partner is not hearing or understanding them. They often believe their partner wants to express his or her feelings and thoughts but is not interested in listening to anyone else's. They may yell things such as "If I could only get it through your thick skull . . ." or cry and complain, "If you'd stop yelling and listen to me for a change."

When people do not feel heard and understood, they often start a fight to get their message across. Rather than being open and listening, each begins to prepare a response while the other is still talking. The harder they try to make themselves heard, the less they are understood and the less appreciated they feel.

5. *The Overfamiliarity Factor* is a couple's attempt to cope with each other's predictable moods and actions. "After all these years, I know you—sometimes better than you know yourself." When said warmly, this may be an affectionate truth and a statement of vintage love. When said curtly, however, it can feel like an insult or a frontal attack designed to silence the other person or to start a fight.

With familiarity comes assumptions couples make about each other. Earned in the past, these assumptions are used in the present to save time and make life predictable. If the assumptions are true and positive, they build a stronger relationship. But if the assumptions are negative, they erode and undercut the relationship and blind those involved so they do not see the positive potential of being together.

6. **The Self-Righteous Factor** springs from the desire to be right and not be made wrong. Some couples engage in open debate to prove they're right. One member wants to reassure him- or herself that he or she is smart and to do this may try to make the partner wrong, as if he or she is stupid. He or she also imagines that all fights are the partner's fault. If the partner would only change, things would get better! By blaming, he or she denies a part in creating conflict and does not see what he or she has done to provoke, invite or manipulate the partner into feeling defensive.

7. **The Loyalty Factor** is rooted in people's need to stand by their commitments to the people they love. Loyalties can play a key role in a relationship and people need to respect and support their partner's loyalties. For example, her loyalties to her parents may be so deep that she would not be willing to move away from them just to please her partner and he needs to understand this. Or his relationship with his children may be so important he may give it first priority in planning weekend activities. By sticking to their commitments, each affirms his or her capacity to be loyal.

A problem arises when one person's loyalty does not fit into a partner's dream or mind-set of how people should act. He treats his kids differently than hers and stands up for them no matter what. She feels betrayed by this.

Loyalty can be the cause of fights when one person is pressured to give up a friendship of many years. She may want to keep seeing her ex-in-laws but her new husband may feel angry because he is jealous or threatened or because she is not willing to take him along when she visits them. So he demands she forget them and side with him. She doesn't want the either-or pressure so she fights to get him to back off his position.

8. ***The Justice Factor*** occurs as one or both persons try to balance the scales of justice of the past. People often remember these resentments for a long time. Somehow they keep echoing in the back of their mind. He may remember how she forgot to phone him when she was out of town. Or she may remember how he was unwilling to stand up to his ex-wife. He may remember when she threatened to leave him and she might remember when he lied to her. Each can have their own list of bad memories that are hard to forget.

People often save these memories like "trading stamps." Each week, month, or year, they may remember a few more inequities and save a few more resentment stamps. The collections continue to build in the back of the person's mind until one day something happens that becomes the straw that broke the camel's back. When this occurs people may show resentment by having a blow-up, a good cry, a period of withdrawal, or some other form of retribution and punishment they feel they deserve.[32]

What makes fights even more chaotic is that one or both parties may be fighting ghosts of the past. His complaints about her may be the same complaints he felt but was unable to express to his mother as a child. The criticisms she has of him may be carry-over resentments echoing from her unexpressed criticisms of her parents or siblings or first husband. People can project any number of faces onto a partner, then get into a big fight as if trying to make up for past inequities.

9. ***The Independence Factor*** stems from the need to define, develop, and express a separate identity. For people to feel satisfied in a long-term relationship, they need to have a sense of their own independence. Few marriages can succeed with

one person always living in the shadow of the other. Neither can endure being trapped in the rut of always agreeing or going along with the other. When this happens and one becomes the leader and the other the follower, eventually both may discover they've gone down the wrong road together or they've gone down the right road with the wrong person. Everyone needs to be his or her own person with separate thoughts, feelings, and opinions.

Independence also comes when people have their own friends and interests. He likes to play tennis Saturday mornings with a couple of buddies, while she likes to be involved in political discussions with her friends over lunch. Separate interests give people activities in which they can get recharged. This gives them a break from each other and helps refill their energy reservoirs. Separate activities also give them something fresh to talk about when they are next together.

But there comes a time when many people develop a stronger need for independence. They want to establish their own identity as different from their partner. They are more willing to do things for themselves and may even fight *against* their partner as a way to determine and define how they want to be instead. "I want to do it *my* way!" Not only that, they want to be applauded and appreciated for their new way of being. So they reject their partner's offerings of support or direction which in times past were wanted, even prized. This change can leave the partner wondering, "What got into him [or her]?"

10. *The Transition Factor* can come into play when things are changing. Couples fight because they are unable to find new solutions to old problems and do not recognize the relationship is going through a transition. The routines developed in the early years of the relationship may no longer work. Giving the same old answers to new questions seems

foolish. New challenges and problems arise and the old solutions are not effective. The old routines have lost their meaning.

In the midst of this transition, couples want to make sure that painful events of the past don't repeat themselves and that things get better in the future, not worse. So to keep control while these changes take place, they try to control each other's behavior. Each tries to make sure that his or her partner will work *for* their dreams and not make things go awry.

This transition factor needs to be recognized for what it is. It doesn't signal the end of the relationship; it can be a new beginning where new ways of responding to each other can be developed.

Exercise: Factors That Influence Your Relationship

When you think of intimate relationships you have been in, how did you deal with some of the factors involved?

Factors	How I Responded	My Partner's Response
1. Desire for excitement		
2. Desire for comfort		

3. Accepting differences

_____

_____

4. Need for appreciation

_____

_____

5. Desire for familiarity

_____

_____

6. Need to be right

_____

_____

7. Loyalty

_____

_____

8. Concern for justice

_____

_____

9. Desire for independence

_____

_____

10. Transition stresses

_____

_____

Is one factor more important than others? How would you number the above list in the order of influence on you?

_____

_____

_____

_____

_____

_____

_____

_____

_____

_____

The Value of Conflict

It is in the heat of the battle that a couple's sense of boundaries are forged. In fights, each lets the other know what he or she is willing to put up with and what is not tolerable. In productive conflicts, each pulls and tugs at each other until new guidelines for the relationship are established that are satisfying to both. When this occurs, the relationship is forced to move ahead and grow instead of staying trapped in old routines that have lost much of their original value.

Another value of the conflict and power struggles is that they provide a chance for each person to open up and express thoughts and feelings that were repressed or ignored because of routines. In the middle of the fight, he may finally tell her what has been bothering him all this time. Or she may finally make it clear that she needs to spend time with him talking about emotional realities if she is to maintain her interest in the relationship.

Conflicts make one point crystal clear to fighting couples after a while. The point is, no matter how much you try, you can't *make* your partner change unless he or she wants to. Each may give in occasionally, but for someone to make a basic change, force is seldom effective. With fighting and force, relationships usually get worse. Accepting this principle and accepting your differences can end the fights or maximize their value.

The Challenges of the Conflict Stage

The challenges of the Conflict stage are numerous. One challenge is for each person to define his or her own personality as different but not separate from the partner's. Another challenge is to learn how to accept a partner's differences. A third challenge is learning how to deal with anger and control in acceptable ways. And a fourth is to discover how to move out of old routines and gain a fresh hold on shared dreams.

Loving couples do fight. But they do it in a way that resolves disagreement rather than creates it. As Ruth put it, "We argue when we need to, and we don't harbor grievances. The air between us is sometimes loud and stormy, but it always clears."

Loving couples learn how to deal with negative emotions and conflict. To begin with, they are seldom or never "brutally honest." They don't express feelings with abandon nor do they say things they would regret later. Criticism, ridicule, and defensiveness only serve to choke the life from a relationship. They know it so they don't express themselves in these ways. They use nonvolatile anger and believe there needs to be a certain restraint (like counting to ten) in conflict. Francine Klagsbrun, after researching one hundred long-married couples concluded that "in a good marriage there's so much trust that each partner can show his weakest side and know he'll still be loved."[33] In these marriages built on trust, neither partner worries about surprise attacks or low blows because they don't do that to each other. They fight fair and take responsibility for their own part of their problems.

Many psychologists have written about procedures couples can follow to have, what George Bach coined, "fair fights."[34] A few basics are worth remembering. Couples need to work out mutually agreeable rules for solving problems *in advance*. They also need to remember that under any complaint is a hidden request that is not verbalized directly but, if discovered, can lead to greater intimacy when responded to in a caring manner. Furthermore, couples need to develop ways to accommodate each other rather than get into direct head-on assaults. And last, they need to break up arguments that are getting too intense by making authentic positive statements.

The Disillusionment Stage

For some couples, there comes a time when enough is enough. They realize there is no way they can force their partner to change. It's no longer worth the battle. Dreams they shared when they first got together became tarnished or obscured by realities, routines, and rage. They feel disenchanted, disappointed and discouraged and say things such as, "I've tried everything I know to make things work out but nothing I do seems to be good enough. I've tried going along with what he says. I've been patient and put up with things. I've tried reasoning, and yelling, and crying, and begging. Nothing seems to work and I've had it!"

When lovers are breaking up, they often experience withdrawal symptoms like crying jags, lack of concentration, eating binges, restlessness yearning for the lost love, and feelings of hopelessness. One or both partners begin to realize that they have grown in different directions and no longer feel as two people walking down the same road. The relationship has progressed to its outer limits, to the point where there is no agreement on major values.

Many relationships experience some disillusionment when values are in conflict. Each partner may begin to wonder, "What happened to the dream? Where did we go wrong? Where do we go from here? Is this how I want to spend the rest of my life?" Sometimes a couple who starts asking these questions feels challenged, more usually they feel a sense of failure. Since most people don't want to feel they have failed, they may give it another try. They may finally take a long vacation together or have a child or build an addition to the house. In one way or another, they attempt to bring new life to a dying relationship.

The Value and Challenges of the Disillusionment Stage

Sometimes it becomes necessary to get to a point of disappointment to break out of old ways of doing things. When couples get to this point, they quit trying to make their partner change to fit their dreams. They confront very serious challenges and choices at this juncture.

The Disillusionment stage is a crucial crossroads. It is the point in which one or both may decide:

1. to stop fighting and give in, pretending everything is fine when in reality it's not

2. to disengage psychologically from the relationship and put their energy elsewhere—such as in work, physical fitness, education, an affair, etc.

3. to get away from the problems by getting out of the relationship

4. to get committed to making things work and transforming the relationship.

One challenge of the Disillusionment stage is to recognize that feelings of discouragement naturally arise from a desire to bring new life to the relationship. If the desire for new life is recognized, a couple can create opportunities for some heart-to-heart talks about their future together.

Another challenge of the Disillusionment stage is to recognize that each person is evolving on a journey toward wholeness and independence and away from looking to a partner for all the love, answers, excitement, support, direction, adoration, or whatever else is missing from life. If this challenge is met, each person begins to take more responsibility for his or her own happiness as well as for the success of their relationship. Transformation is possible.

The Transformation Stage

Many people decide to hang in there with their partner. Their relationship may have been side-tracked by routines and conflicts; they may have lost touch with each other, but that doesn't mean the relationship isn't right. They are determined to make it a success! In spite of everything, they believe in the possibility of change and transformation.

When something is transformed, it is changed in form, appearance, and/or function. For a relationship to be transformed, it needs to age like wine so the bitterness is gone and the special qualities become more appreciable. Romantic dreams need to be revised and made more practical. Midcourse adjustments to each other's routines are necessary. Even some conflict can be part of the transformation process and useful to help define the rules, roles, and boundaries of the relationship. All of this calls for a commitment because to pull this off, couples need to be willing to transform their relationship from a young romance to a long-lasting love.

Transforming a relationship requires that a couple take their old relationship and give it new life with new form, appearance, and function. You can't do it alone and you can't expect your partner to do it all either. A joint effort is necessary, effort that is made without resentment and without keeping tally of how much each is doing. It's possible to do this and enjoy each other in the process.

Enjoying Each Other

One of the characteristics of couples who enjoy each other is that they like to have fun together. They tend to respond rapidly when they spot the playful spirit in the other. Both feel free to be themselves and do not feel required to inhibit their excitement and enthusiasm. They also share a spontaneity that creates an adventuresome spirit. Rather than getting bored with each other as time goes by, they become more enraptured and enchanted by each other and the times they share. Their emotional closeness continues to regenerate itself without requiring unreasonable effort.

Happy couples spend many hours together by choice. They are not clones with identical likes and dislikes, but they do have a core of similar pleasures that they find joy in sharing. They often would rather spend time with their partner than with anyone else. Jeannette and Robert Lauer, researchers in this field, state that a couple's "intense intimacy—their preference for shared rather than separate activities—seems to reflect a richness and fulfillment in the relationship rather than a loss of identity."[35]

Couples who enjoy their relationship also have a sincere interest in the interests of each other, even after many years. Though not caught up in a whirlpool of excitement, they still recognize the fascination they had for each other when they first got together. They continue to be curious about one another, surprised by new aspects of their partner which surface from time to time. Loving couples report that they still feel thrilled and honored to be together.[36]

Knowing these stages of development many relationships go through, you can more easily predict the future of your relationship. With all this in mind, you are ready to make your final decision!

Chapter 8

❦❦❦

MAKING YOUR FINAL DECISION

"I'm at that point where I either go for it, or I get out of the relationship. I'm nervous. It feels like the most important decision in my life. How can I really know if I'm making the right one?"

"She keeps pushing. She wants me to marry her, but I'm still not sure. I've tried making lists of the pros and cons but they don't seem to help. They only confuse me more. How can I decide?"

"Let's do it! Let's get married tomorrow! I love you and that ought to be enough. That's all we need, isn't it?"

"My married friends tell me my doubts are just last minute jitters. My single friends tell me they are the voice of my inner self and I should pay attention to them. I don't know what to think!"

E ventually the time comes when you are ready to make your final decision—to go for it or to bail out! This chapter presents a strategy you can use to make sure your decision is the right one. Whereas some people rely mostly on their emotions to decide, others primarily rely on their convictions, and still others think of the practicalities of the matter. In this chapter, you will discover ways of making your final decision and using all of these aspects of yourself. Included here is a consideration of some delicate realities people who have been married before need to contemplate before deciding on a lifelong commitment to a new relationship.

There are some useful guidelines you can use to help you feel confident that you are making the right decision. Your feelings can be an important indicator. If you find yourself feeling more hopeful, relaxed, friendly, alive, and joyful, then your relationship obviously is encouraging feelings worth having. If you find yourself thinking more positively about the future, analyzing your shared realities with a strong sense of honesty, being curious about your future, and hungry for more knowledge about yourselves and life, you're on the right track. These are the kinds of thoughts that will keep your relationship alive and growing.

"Who" in You Decides?

Perhaps you still have doubts about your ability to make a good choice. If so, it's natural for you to want to be sure.

Think back to the interview in Chapter 5. You learned about the personality concept of ego states and how to interview each ego state in a potential partner. Now consider your own ego states so you can discover "who" in you is making your decision. Each of your ego states influences how you pick a partner as well as how you make your final decision and which partner to pick. Your decision needs to be made at a feeling level (Child), at a conviction level (Parent), and at a practical level (Adult).

If you are already sure of your decision, you might find your different ego states having an imaginary conversation with your partner:

Feeling level (Child): "I know I love you and that you're right for me because I feel so good when we're together!"

Conviction level (Parent): "I believe we'll make it together because we have the same values."

Practical level (Adult): "I think we will succeed because we set goals, make decisions, and solve problems effectively."

When all parts of you agree, it's ideal. But you may not have a unanimous vote inside yourself. Part of you may be in favor of the relationship while another part may be wanting something more. If you're not so sure, you might think: "I love her (feeling level), but I don't love her kids (conviction level), and I'm not sure I want to be a father again (practical level)." A different person might have other issues that interfere with a unanimous vote and think: "I love him (feeling level), but I won't marry him because he's too insecure (practical level), and I need to take care of myself first (conviction level)."

You need to pay attention to each one of your ego states. One or two of your ego states is not enough. If you don't consider each ego state, you will have created a situation in which sooner or later either you or your partner will question the relationship and perhaps end up dissatisfied or heartbroken. Using each of your three ego states will help you feel confident that your decision is the best one for you. If you are aware of each ego state and there is disagreement between your feelings, convictions, and practical observations, this is a *potential* problem. It does not have to hold you back if you decide to resolve your doubts.

The Feeling Level

Love is experienced by the inner Child as a passionate, romantic, dreamy feeling. Naturally, many people want to feel this and when they do, they often become convinced that this means they have found the right person (and they very well may have!) They imagine that their feelings are proof of a long-lasting love.

The Child in you is important because it's the part of you who feels thrilled to be with the one you love. It is also the Child in you that can feel disenchanted if things don't go the way you want them to.

Some people make decisions only from their Child ego state. Since the Child is the part of our personality that both feels and adapts to circumstances, the Child's decisions when excited and in love may be impulsive, convenient, or protective.

Impulsive decisions are made without regard for the future. They are made on the spur of the moment with only immediate gratification in mind. "If it feels good, do it." Some people make the decision to get married this way. They rush off in a moment when defenses are low or illusions high and they wake up days or years later to find themselves sorry for what they got themselves into.

Convenient decisions are made by people who decide to go along with whatever seems easiest at the time. They may not have a highly emotional investment in the situation. They may go along with others, attempting to be pleasing and seldom saying no. Some people stay in "going nowhere" relationships because, "it's better than nothing." For example, Charlene is dating a married man. He has told her that in three to four years, after his kids go off to college, he will get a divorce. She knows the relationship has no future, but she keeps seeing him anyway. She enjoys his attention. She doesn't take responsibility for shaping her own life; she passively accepts a situation that may ultimately prove unsatisfying.

Are You The One For Me?

Rachel recalled: "I didn't love him at first. But he loved me and took good care of me. It felt good to go out and to have someone to do things with. After a while, I began to get hooked on his attention. I looked forward to his phone calls and his cards in the mail. As time passed, I guess I became so used to him that I fooled myself into thinking that I was in love with him."

Protective decisions are made when a person places his or her own security needs above all other considerations. These people are often basically hopeful that they pick partners who they believe will protect them in one way or another. Perhaps he or she will be a good parent to their children or give them the financial security they never had, help them feel safe instead of scared in social situations, or be someone who will never leave them. These kinds of protective decisions may be made for the very high price of giving up a personal sense of identity or the excitement of a life lived with more risks and deeper meaning.

Although passionate love is desirable and necessary, it is not enough. Feelings need to be balanced and guided by clear values and accurate information for the relationship to flourish and succeed. To make your final decision wisely, you need to wait to consider what the other parts of you have to say. The Child in you needs to be given only 33 percent of your final decision vote. The exercise on p. 172 can help you clarify your inner-Child feeling.

If you let your Child make the final decision, sooner or later your Adult will start asking uncomfortable questions, and your Parent will become critical and judgmental. Since many marriages are decided using only the feeling level and the statistics of divorce are about 50 percent, it is important to pay attention to your values and information as well.[37]

The Conviction Level

The Parent in you plays an important part in your decision making process. It is the part of you that has values and beliefs

Exercise: Assessing Your Feelings

To find out what your inner Child wants, here are some questions that can help you clarify your feelings. To answer them put a check in the column that best matches your feelings.

	Yes	No	Maybe/ Sometimes
1. Do I really love this person?	_____	_____	_____
2. Do I enjoy spending quiet time with him/her?	_____	_____	_____
3. Do we have fun doing things together?	_____	_____	_____
4. Can I trust him/her?	_____	_____	_____
5. Do I feel secure with him/her?	_____	_____	_____
6. Will he/she be able to take care of me if I get sick, tired, or sad?	_____	_____	_____
7. Is there anything about his/her personality that scares me or makes me feel uncomfortable?	_____	_____	_____
8. Is there anything about him/her that I don't like?	_____	_____	_____
9. Is he/she hiding anything from me?	_____	_____	_____
10. Do I feel he/she loves me but wants me to change?	_____	_____	_____
11. Am I choosing this person because I feel I ought to?	_____	_____	_____

To find your Child compatibility score, add the following way: For questions 1 through 6, each "Yes" answer is worth 3 points, each "Maybe/Sometimes" 2 points, each "No" 1 point. For questions 7 through 11, the scoring pattern is reversed. Each "No" is worth 3 points, each "Maybe or Sometimes" 2 points, and each "Yes" 1 point.

Now total your answers. (A total of 33 points is possible.) If you have between 26 and 33 points, it means the Child in you is feeling good about the relationship and wants to choose this person. If you have scored between 17 to 25 points, your inner Child is not too sure if the relationship is right for you. If you scored 16 points or less, you really need to think about it; your inner Child is not very hopeful or secure.

about people, life, marriage, sex, etc. Your values guide much of your behavior and provide a sense of direction to your life. They are hard to change; they have the capacity to bring great strength or great conflict to your relationship. Therefore it is essential that you consider your Parent ego stage in your final decision.

Be sure that the basic values about life and love that you and your potential partner hold are similar. They don't have to be identical, but the closer they are, the less conflict you will have. If they are alike, you will find it easy to agree and appreciate each other and not lock horns trying to get your partner to see things your way. You will have a strong base to work from.

Some people make their decisions using *only* their Parent ego state. They say things like "I *ought* to marry this person because it's what all my friends and family expect me to do." Or, "I *should* get married and he is a nice enough guy." These people are usually basing their decisions on what others think. They carry their parents' opinions in their heads and are unable to take a stand and decide for themselves what they feel or think much less want. Rene explained how she made her decision to marry Michael: "My friends all liked him and said I'd be a fool to let him get away. And my parents treated him like a son. They said he would be a good husband and a good father. I wasn't sure, but I listened to them. They have always been right so I decided he must be right for me."

Sometimes a person's inner Parent has negative convictions and says, "Nothing will ever turn out right, with that person" or "You need to pick someone with the same religious traditions, someone who will fit into the family better." These examples of negative parental convictions need examination. They may be old stereotypes, messages, or mind-sets that can be changed.

If the Parent part of you makes the final decision against what the Child in you wants, your Child will feel neglected. A relationship based primarily on "oughts" and "shoulds," tends to become static, boring, and unsatisfying with time. Sooner or later you will begin to question the validity of the relationship.

Exercise: **How Similar Are Your Values?**

To check out if your Parent ego state is in control of your decision, ask yourself the following questions. Place a check in the appropriate column.

	Yes	No	Sort of/ Maybe
Are your beliefs similar regarding:			
1. The importance of religion	___	___	___
2. Having and raising children	___	___	___
3. Saving and spending money	___	___	___
4. Types of vacations	___	___	___
5. Sex	___	___	___
6. The necessity for education	___	___	___
7. Work attitudes and career planning	___	___	___

To score: Give yourself 2 points for every "Yes" answer, 1 point for every "Sort of/Maybe," and no points for "No" answers. If most of your answers were "Yes," you will have a lot of parental values in common. If many of your answers were "Sort of/Maybe" or "No," you may find you have some important differences that could become a problem if they were not resolved early in the relationship.

Exercise: What Does Your Inner Parent Advise?

Chances are you will agree on some issues and not on others. You need to consider the following questions to find out if your convictions agree with your feelings.

Answer the following questions by placing a check next to the answer that you believe is most accurate.

	Yes	No	Sort of/ Maybe
1. Will I be able to live with him/her if our beliefs are different?	___	___	___
2. Do I value being with my partner more than being with other people?	___	___	___
3. Does he/she value being with me more than being with other people or doing other activities?	___	___	___
4. Will I be able to take care of my partner if he/she is sick?	___	___	___
5. Will I be able to take care of my partner if he/she is tired?	___	___	___
6. Will I be able to take care of my partner if he/she is sad?	___	___	___
7. Will I be able to handle it if he/she acts needy?	___	___	___
8. Will I be able to handle it if he/she acts bossy?	___	___	___
9. Will our parents and families approve of our union?	___	___	___
10. If our cultural or subcultural backgrounds are different, will we cope with the differences?	___	___	___

To score: Each "Yes" answer is worth 2 points, each "Sort of/Maybe 1 point, and each "No" 0 points. (A total of 20 points is possible for this section.)

Now add your scores from this and the previous exercise. If you have between 26 and 34 points, it means your values are similar enough and your inner Parent approves of this person as the right person for you. If your score is from 17 to 25 points, your Parent ego state is not so sure about the relationship. If you score 16 points or less, your values and beliefs are too different and you will likely have major conflicts if you don't resolve them. You might be wise to consider limiting your relationship to a good friendship.

The Practical Level

Long-lasting love requires a practical approach. Spontaneity, positive intentions, and shared values are important but a couple needs to be practical to handle all the challenges that marriage presents. The inner Adult is concerned with information, facts, skills, plans, and so forth. When a person evaluates the relationship with the Adult ego state, he or she is able to see beyond the aura of passion and good wishes to the nitty-gritty of daily living. Therefore, to make your final decision, it is essential that you use your inner Adult.

People who tend to make their decisions *only* from their Adult ego state are very rational and consider what's convenient and appropriate. They may have many areas of agreement—such as paying the bills on time, keeping things orderly in the attic, taking the car in to be maintained regularly, etc.—which makes life easy. But if they marry and have considered only their Adult, they are likely to have difficulty understanding the more emotional and illogical aspects of feelings as well as their partner's strongly held values. Chances are they may not laugh often or have much fun together, nor will they be very passionate or tender and "in tune" with each other emotionally.

Exercise: How Practical Is Your Relationship?

Place a check next to the answer that you think is most appropriate.

	Yes	No	Sometimes/ Maybe
1. Is he/she responsible?	_____	_____	_____
2. Do we get along most of the time?	_____	_____	_____
3. Will we be able to grow together?	_____	_____	_____
4. Will we be able to deal with disagreements?	_____	_____	_____
5. Is he or she able to keep contracts and promises?	_____	_____	_____
6. Do we communicate well?	_____	_____	_____
7. Are we committed to the relationship?	_____	_____	_____
8. Do I feel accepted by my partner?	_____	_____	_____
9. Do I accept my partner as he/she is?	_____	_____	_____
10. Do I generally understand my partner?	_____	_____	_____
11. Does my partner generally understand me?	_____	_____	_____

To score: Each "Yes" is worth 3 points, each "Maybe/Sometimes" 2 points, each "No" 1 point. (A total of 33 points is possible.) If you have scored between 26 and 33 points, your practical Adult considers it to be a good choice. If you scored between 18 and 25 points, your Adult may be still thinking about whether or not to get involved. If you have scored 16 points or less, it's a sign that warns you against getting involved with this person.

Your Relationship Compatibility

Now add your scores from all of the exercises. They could add up to a maximum of 100 points. Use the following chart as a guideline for making your final decision. Although no test such as this can be considered infallible, it can help you put your decision-making into focus.

80 to 100 points	Great relationship! Go for it!
65 to 79 points	It may work, with some adjustments.
50 to 64 points	It may be good, but it's probably not right for you.
0 to 49 points	Get out now while you still can.

Being in Agreement with Yourself

When people bring their three ego states into agreement, they make decisions that have a clear intention in mind. Their decisions are not made by habit or happenstance; they are made because they believe wholly in what they are doing. These decisions have heart and integrity.

Intentional decisions are a mark of maturity. Someone who has an important dream and a well-thought-out plan is more likely to succeed in life. They make intentional decisions because they are goal-oriented, trying to create the kind of world and lifestyles that they believe in. They are made by people who take life and love seriously.

Exploring Your Decision

There are several questions that don't fit simply into a "yes-no" format but can shed further light on your decision. They basically evaluate your relationship more than your partner.

1. How well do we solve problems and handle our differences with each other?

2. How will we handle nonnegotiable or irreconcilable differences? (For example, if I'm a pet lover and my partner is not, will I be able to be happy without a pet? Or will my partner be willing to have a pet?)

3. What are the strengths of our relationship?

4. What are the weaknesses of our relationship?

5. What promises have we made to each other? Are they likely to come true?

6. What challenges will we face if we stick together?

7. What will be easy about being together? What will be not so easy about being together?

8. What makes me think the relationship will last?

These questions raise some issues that can make or break a relationship. Remember, the more you know in advance, the less you will regret later.

What Do You Hear Yourself Saying?

"Yes" can be scary to say when you think about the risks and consequences of your decision. Saying "yes" can also be a relief, that finally you've found someone and even more, you've decided to go for it. You are ready to start your journey together and you can feel your excitement and dedication mount.

If you have listened to your convictions, feelings, and practical sides to help you decide, you can be confident that whatever decision you have made is right for you. You have analyzed in what areas you and your partner will be able to get along, as well as your areas of conflict. If you know in advance what you are getting into, your chances of working things out in hard times will be in your favor. You can count on both your partner's and your own ability to handle tough issues as well as good ones.

If you have decided that "No, this is not the right person for me," believe yourself. You have given it thought and time, and if you think the person or the relationship is not right for you, then it's not.

If you are not convinced about the relationship and your answer is "Maybe" or "I'm Not Sure," then wait. Don't rush into a situation that you may later regret. Give yourself more time. Wait six months. Wait another six if necessary. Pay attention to how things develop and to what you feel, think, and believe. If you still can't make a decision after a reasonable period of time, maybe it's time to look elsewhere. He or she may be a lovable and good person—but not the right one for you.

Listening to Your Inner Voice

Sometimes people find themselves in a situation where they want to commit themselves to the relationship but a deep inner voice keeps warning them not to. Many people trust this inner voice and follow its lead. Others do not. They ignore it because they imagine it to just be a case of the last-minute jitters. For example, Karen looking back on her first marriage, admitted, "Just before we got married we moved to the West Coast. While driving across the country I can still remember thinking to myself, I don't think it's going to work out. But I didn't want to listen to myself. I wish I had. I would have saved us both a lot of pain."

Your inner voice is often the voice of wisdom and caution. It may be the rational part that questions the relationship, or the emotional part of oneself that can sense and forecast eventual dissatisfaction. If you're not right for each other, you'll likely sense this.

There is one caution, however. Listen to your inner voice to make sure it's yours and not one left over from childhood or a previous relationship. If it is a statement your parents used to say, double check that it is true for you today. As Robert recalled when his relationship ended after months of struggle, "I listened to an inner voice that said, 'You can do anything you want to do.' That was not true. I couldn't make it work out."

To be sure your inner voice is speaking what's true for you, use your feelings to confirm it. If you are feeling relaxed and confident, positive and with a sense of inner peace, your feelings are in agreement with your inner voice. But if you find yourself feeling anxious, hesitant, disinterested, or confused, slow down and find out why before you take the leap. Your emotions and body reactions may surface before your mind becomes aware of your discomfort.

If you notice negative behaviors cropping up in yourself or your partner, they may be yellow flags. Being critical, flippant, or discounting; being unwilling to talk about important concerns; ignoring or mistreating people, possessions, or pets; having serious sexual dysfunction; acting in embarrassing ways in public—all are signals of "Caution, Proceed with Care." They may foretell some irreconcilable differences.

Tough Realities Make for Tough Decisions

There are many kinds of tough realities. Two important ones today are those of being a blended family and of being a two-income family.

There are often important differences between two people's dreams and realities. When personalities or lifestyles clash, the decision to love and live with someone is a tough one. Two-career families face a long list of challenges. If both partners are at work from 8 A.M. to 6 P.M., they come home tired to face an onslaught of other chores. This pace is bound to lead to stress. Can they handle this extra stress? What if one person is asked to move for business reasons; will the other be ready, willing, and able? If one person works day shift and the other swing shift or graveyard shift, when do they get to see each other?

For example, one couple struggled with their final decision: she wanted to stay in a small community where she had many close friends and he wanted to move to the city where he could pursue his career and have more excitement around him. They loved each other but were stuck at the dilemma: Who would give up their friends and lifestyle for the other?

The many blended families of today present new realities and decisions not necessary in the past. Children—mine, yours, and ours—present many problems. It can be very hard if it is necessary to move away from the kids or if the ex-spouse has custody and moves.

Financial obligations to previous partners can have a major impact on a relationship. Steve had been married before. In the divorce settlement, his ex-wife kept the house so she could raise their three children. He was required to pay 50 percent of his monthly salary in child support. This didn't leave him much to live on, but this was not a big problem for him—until he met Shannon. If they went for dinner, she would always have to pay her way. When they wanted to go away for a weekend, he wouldn't be able to afford it. Shannon loved him but was hesitant to marry him. She didn't want to live like that for the next fifteen years.

Another tough reality is when partners love each other but not their partner's kids. Doreen has two children, ages 6 and 8. Daniel's children have already grown and gone off to college. If Daniel doesn't want to take on the tasks of child-rearing, can their relationship make it? Daniel and Doreen decided to stay together and work through their differences in relation to the children. It wasn't easy for them to establish clear roles. They made arrangements about when they would all relate as a family with the children, and when they were to be alone as a couple. Another couple in a similar situation decided that it was not worth the effort. They split up, married other people, yet continued an affair with each other until one day they got caught and had many more tough decisions to make.

For couples who have children and want to become a new family, there are other realities that can make the decision far more complex. If either of you have been married before, then ask yourself:

- Where will we live, my place or yours?

- Will your children or mine live with us?

- Will they come and visit on weekends? If so, how and when will that be decided and handled?

- Will we have more children?

- What role will I play with your children, and vice versa? Do you expect me to be a parent, friend, disciplinarian, savior? How will I feel in that role? How will you feel if I don't want that role?

- What kind of treatment can I expect from your children? And from you as their parent and as my spouse?

- How will their visits affect our life? How might they enhance our lives? How might they limit or interfere with our lives?

- How much child and/or spouse support do I pay? How much does he or she pay? For how long? How will that affect our budget? Will it mean we can't go on vacations or out on weekends, or buy clothes, furniture, a car or a home?

- How much will my partner's ex-spouse or mine interfere with our lives? How much will my ex-spouse be a problem for you?

- How will discipline issues with the children be handled? How will you feel if I discipline your children? How will I respond if you discipline my children? Will it create two teams around the house—your team (with you and your children) and my team (with me and mine)?

- How will the chores around the house be handled? Who will do what? Will one of us have to push the other(s) to get things done?

The Final Checklist

Given the enormity of your decision, it might seem as if you could go on and on asking yourself questions to be sure of something that is impossible to guarantee. The following questions can short cut this process and point you in the right direction.

1. Are we ready?

2. Do we have a clear sense of what kind of future we want to create for ourselves?

3. Are we willing to make the most of our differences?

4. Do we have what it takes to weather the seasons of marriage?

5. Do we have support systems we can reach for when things get tough?

6. Are we both committed to learning more about what makes marriages last and committed to making ours last?

Last-Minute Doubts

Awareness sometimes leads to doubts. The more you know, the more you question. Like first-year medical students who worry that they have each new disease they read about, you may notice some gaps in your relationship and begin to question if you've made a mistake and if it's possible to ever find the right person. As you become comfortable thinking about the more practical aspects of love, and in seeing your relationship from its many facets, you will see the value of these questions.

Once you make a final decision, you might become confused about whether or not you have made the right choice. You may wonder, "Is there a better catch out there for me? Am I making my decision the right way?" You may feel puzzled by still feeling loyal or attracted to someone else. Or you may be perplexed by the promises you made or the façades you've worn and want to discard. Ambivalence and conflict may emerge.

For some people, just having thoughts of doubt causes enormous anxiety. However, doubt is natural. In fact, it is common and predictable. It is an important test for any relationship. When people have doubts, they often put their partner through a series of subtle tests to find out what's really true.

Testing occurs in over 35 percent of the romantic relationships, according to research done by Leslie Baxter and William Wilmot.[38] These researchers found that women were more likely to test relationships through indirect means than men and that there are various types of tests lovers use. Testing the other person's limits is the most common type of test. It is as if the person is asking, "How much will he or she put up with and what can I get away with and still keep this person around and interested?" Of those sampled, 33 percent admitted they tested by making their partner jealous. Some used more subtle means such as expressing mildly self-deprecating statements (in hopes that the partner would disagree) or by touching on sensitive topics (to see how the partner would react). Another type of test some people use is to ask the partner to choose between the relationship and something else, like going skiing or visiting parents. In spite of the tension testing creates—and the conflict or disappointment it can lead to—it is often an important part of the final decision process. However, some couples decide to break up as a result of testing.

Something's Bound to Go Wrong

People who have been hurt too many times, or even one important time, often become cautious. To protect themselves from more hurt, they pull back at just the last moment. Their disappointments have left them doubtful that their dreams will ever come true. "Something is bound to go wrong. It always does. My dream didn't work out before; why should I imagine that it might work out this time?" They don't allow themselves to get hopeful lest they get disappointed again. Mentally and emotionally replaying these past pains and future fears only keeps them away from someone who could love them well.

If this is true for you, you need to learn how to break this self-defeating cycle. You need to *focus your attention on the possible instead of on the painful.* See your past in its proper perspective: of course some people have disappointed you. That may have been painful. But don't give up your dreams because of previous letdowns.

In spite of the possibility of a future disappointment, it *is* worth the risk of loving again. Start to program yourself with an expectation that you *will* succeed and in the long run you will get what you want.

Become willing to take the risk to be vulnerable, even to surrender to love and let your new dreams guide your life again. Trust that you will make a good decision and that you know how to do it. Whatever the future may bring, have faith that you will be able to handle it.

The Bad News and the Good News

"To get from Point A to Point B, you have to leave Point A." Letting go of being single in favor of the unknown—a new and committed relationship—is a big challenge. Your decision to love will have a long-lasting effect on you and your loved ones. For some, the decision is easy; for others, it's quite hard. How can you be sure you've thought of everything and won't get surprised in the future?

Even when you take the time to examine yourself and your relationship beforehand, there are no guarantees. People and relationships change with time and in unpredictable ways. That's the bad news. But the *good news* is that well-meaning people making informed and committed decisions have a greater chance of making their relationship a success.

Trust Yourself

Now that you have considered your relationship from many directions and have ways to analyze your perspectives, let yourself decide. Decide in whatever way is most right for you. You may want to go to some quiet place outdoors where your mind can feel free. Or you may want to write your thoughts down on paper and organize them so your decision becomes more obvious. Or you may want to pray, asking for the strength to discern what is right and true for you. Create the environment that works best for you to make an important decision. Then meditate on it, examine it, question it, even talk about it—and then when you're ready—trust yourself, make your decision, and stick by it!

Chapter 9

THE RIGHT RELATIONSHIP WITH THE RIGHT PARTNER

Living with the right partner is to really live well. It is to really be together and "encounter" each other in "genuine dialogue."[39] Much of what passes for dialogue is not. It is merely trite conversation or trying to convince another of something or only listening to one's own voice. In moments of genuine dialogue, each person has the other in mind; each is "all there" with the other, not thinking of something or someone else. In dialogue, couples talk *with* each other, not at or past each other. They look at each other; they do not close their eyes or look at the ceiling or floor. They look at and speak directly to the other without evading or diluting the issue. They really listen, instead of planning what they are going to say when their partner stops talking. To find and continue with the right partner requires a decision that genuine dialogue is necessary to keep a relationship alive and vibrant.

A Dialogic Relationship

Genuine dialogue creates a dialogic relationship in which each person gives his or her all to the partner. To give oneself does not mean forfeiting one's identity, nor getting lost or swallowed up in the feelings, thoughts, dreams, or activities of the other. To give oneself is to live with one's own standpoint and that of the partner in mind also. It means to validate, from deep within, the value and wisdom of your partner's world, acknowledging that it is of equal significance and importance as your own. This kind of giving is an art. But we are all potential artists. As philosopher-theologian Martin Buber points out, "There are no gifted or un-gifted, only those who give themselves and those who withhold themselves."[40]

For there to be a sense of dialogue, there needs to be open communication and a feeling of trust, a climate that allows both people to tell each other, as they never have before, what's really going on in their minds and emotions. In this kind of open communication, there is a willingness to express thoughts and feelings, wishes and needs as accurately as possible and to listen carefully when the other does the same. It is expressing what is true at your deepest levels, talking from your heart and wanting to understand the truths your partner is also expressing.

Besides speaking clearly and listening intently, dialogue requires both *understanding* and *empathy*. Generally, understanding has to do with knowing, empathy with feeling. In a committed relationship, understanding involves getting into each other's minds; empathy, into each other's feelings. With understanding and empathy, each person develops a sense of what is important to the other and why a partner does what he or she does.

Acceptance is another underpinning of a dialogic relationship. Loving couples acknowledge their partner's flaws but believe their positive qualities are more important than their differences. One clinician refers to this as "the ability to continue idealizing the loved one while seeing him or her clearly, and even negatively at times."[41]

Acceptance is more than treating your partner with the same courteous attention that extends to casual acquaintances or a boss. Each partner needs to accept each other on that person's own terms, without trying to change or make the other person into a different person. In doing this, both come to realize that their differences can compliment rather than undermine the relationship. And with a sense of appreciation comes a deep respect for being invited into such a hallowed sanctuary as the partner's feelings, thoughts, dreams, and life. As Simone de Beauvoir once wrote, "Respect each other's privacy and deal gently with each other's dreams."[42] Loving couples take this saying as a matter of course with each other.

Respect for another person becomes dialogic when there is also self-respect. This sense of self-respect comes from three basic attitudes, according to management specialists Warren Bennis and Burt Nanus.[43] First, a person needs to acknowledge their own strengths without blocking themselves with worries of vanity or humility. In doing this, they also need to acknowledge and accept their weaknesses as real, but not as fatal flaws. Secondly, they need to nurture and develop their strengths and to compensate for their imperfections before they become perilous to others. Third, they need to exercise their capacity to modify the fit between their personal strengths and the needs of the relationship and their partner at any point in time. This means that they use their strengths and weaknesses as "raw ingredients," which they blend to make their relationship last.

A Lasting Commitment

Loving couples aren't quitters. They have a commitment to their partner and to their relationship. They have a willingness to be unhappy for a while and a determination to work through the hard times. Hugh spoke of his marriage in these terms, "I'm secure in knowing that even if there are tough times ahead, we'll still stick together." His partner, Ann, chimed in with, "We're really right for each other. Our lives and dreams fit together."

Shared dreams that bring a couple together originally are also what keep them together over the long run. Loving couples maintain their shared dreams. They continue to work for mutual goals, even as their relationship and their dreams evolve. In doing so, they keep themselves looking ahead to new possibilities. They continue to experience, over and over, that they are choosing a future they both want to share.

Loving couples realize that there are no magic formulas or secret recipes. Loving requires a fusion of a serious commitment to each other and to solving problems as they arise. It also requires a relaxed attitude toward day-by-day challenges that come up, an acceptance of the past and an optimism about the future, and a union of work and play. This commitment is one that lasts, in plenty and in want, in sickness and in health, through thick and thin, in moments of unhappiness and in years of joy.

Chapter Notes

1. Life dreams are seldom mentioned per se by psychologists, in spite of their central importance in people's behavior. However, several of the more dynamic theorists seem to be thinking in similar directions.

Daniel Levinson, in his seminal book on the adult development of men, includes dreams as central to his conception of a person's basic life structure. See Levinson, D., et al., *The Seasons of a Man's Life*, New York: Ballantine Books, 1978, pp. 91–94.

Charles Garfield, an expert on high achievement, uses the terms "mission" and "vision" in a way almost synonymous to our concept of "dreams." See Garfield, C., *Peak Performance*, Los Angeles: Jeremy Tarcher, Inc., 1984, pp. 61-80; and Garfield, C., *Peak Performers: The New Heroes of American Business*, New York: Morrow, 1986.

Gordon Allport, one of the founding fathers of modern psychology, refers to a future orientation: "The possession of long-range goals, regarded as central to one's personal existence, distinguishes the human being from the animal, the adult from the child, and in many cases the healthy personality from the sick." Allport, G., *Becoming*, New Haven: Yale University Press, 1955, p. 51.

Existential psychologist Rollo May agrees, stating that the future "is the dominant mode of time for human beings . . . Personality can only be understood as we see it on a trajectory toward the future . . ." May, R., in Friedman, M., ed., *The Worlds of Existentialism: A Critical Reader*, New York: Random House, 1964, p. 450.

Abraham Maslow, one of the leaders in humanistic and transpersonal psychology, also writes of this future-oriented perspective. See Maslow, A., *Toward a Psychology of Being*, New York: Van Nostrand, 1962.

Philosopher Jose Ortega y Gasset also believed that "one lives toward the future . . . and [each person] is a project, something which is not yet but aspires to be." Ortega y Gasset, J., in Friedman, M., ed., *The Worlds of Existentialism: A Critical Reader*, New York: Random House, 1964, pp. 117, 154.

This is echoed by the theologian-psychologist Robert Leslie who believes, "Life can be pulled by goals just as surely as it can be pushed by drives." Leslie, R., *Jesus and Logotherapy*, Nashville: Abingdon Press, 1965, p. 52.

Sister Corita Kent and Father John Pintaro add another perspective: "Maybe we are less than our dreams, but that would make us more than some gods would dream of." Kent, C. and Pintaro, J., *To Believe In Man*, New York: Harper & Row, 1970.

The famous physician Hans Selye believed that "'Realistic people' who pursue 'practical aims' are rarely as realistic or practical, in the long run of life, as the dreamers who pursue their dreams." He believes that this pursuit of one's dreams is what brings a *joie de vivre*. Selye, H., *Stress Without Distress*, New York: New American Library, 1975, p. 79; and Selye, H., *The Stress of Life*, New York: McGraw-Hill, 1978.

And this dream of the future is what Martin Luther King, Jr. spoke of when he called the nation to account and to action in his memorialized "I Have a Dream" speech, delivered in Washington, D.C., on August 28, 1963. Following Dr. King's death, Dr. Ralph Abernathy, President of the Southern Christian Leadership Conference, remarked that "they have killed the dreamer, but they have *not* killed the dream." Motown record jacket #5340ML.

2. Andersen, S., and Bem, S., "Sex Typing and Androgyny in Dyadic Interaction: Individual Differences in Responsiveness to Physical Attractiveness," *Journal of Personality and Social Psychology*, 41, 1981, pp. 74–86; and Wakil, S., "Campus Mate Selection Preferences: A Cross-Cultural Comparison," *Social Forces*, 51, 1973, pp. 471–476.

3. Analysis of personal statements found on the video previews at a suburban video dating service in the San Francisco Bay area done by the authors.

4. Gilligan, C., *In a Different Voice*, Cambridge, Mass.: Harvard University Press, 1982.

5. Levinson, D., *The Seasons of a Man's Life*, New York: Ballantine Books, 1978; Sheehy, G., *Passages: Predictable Crises of Adult Life*, New York: E. P. Dutton, 1976; Davitz, L., "My Ideal Woman," *McCall's*, July 1985, pp. 80f; and informal research by the authors.

6. Frankl, V., "Existence and Values," in Leslie, R., *Jesus and Logotherapy*, Nashville: Abingdon Press, 1965, p. 29; and Frankl, V., *The Doctor and the Soul*, New York: Bantam Books, 1967, p. xii. See also Frankl, V., *Man's Search for Meaning*, New York: Washington Square Press, 1965.

7. For more on schemata and frames of reference, see Beck, A., *Depression: Causes and Treatment*, Philadelphia: University of Pennsylvania Press, 1970; Berne, E., *What Do You Do After You Say Hello*, New York: Grove Press, 1972; Bower, G., et al., "Scripts in Memory for Text," *Cognitive Psychology*, 1979, Vol. 11, pp. 177–220; Fiske, S., and Linville, P., "What Does the Schema Concept Buy Us?"

Personality and Social Psychology Bulletin, 1980, Vol. 6, pp. 543–557; Fiske, S., and Taylor, S., *Social Cognition*, Reading, Mass.: Addison-Wesley, 1983; Hastie, R., "Schematic Principles in Human Memory," in Higgins, E., Herman, C., and Zanna, M., eds., *Social Cognition*, Hillsdale, N.J.: Erlbaum, 1981; Hastie, R., and Kumar, P., "Person Memory: Personality Traits as Organizing Principles in Memory for Behavior," *Journal of Personality and Social Psychology*, 1979, Vol. 37, pp. 25–38.

8. For more on the impact of relatives, especially grandparents, on developing mind-sets, see James, J., "Grandparents and the Family Script Parade," *Transactional Analysis Journal*, January 1984, Vol. 14, No. 1, pp. 18–28.

9. For more on cultural influences on mind-sets, see Campbell, D., "On the Conflicts Between Biological and Social Evolution and Between Psychology and Moral Tradition," *American Psychologist*, December 1975, pp. 1103–1125; James, J., "Cultural Consciousness: The Challenge to TA," *Transactional Analysis Journal*, Vol. 13, No. 4, October 1983, pp. 207–216; James, M., "Cultural Scripts: Historical Events vs. Historical Interpretation," *Transactional Analysis Journal*, Vol. 13, No. 4, October 1983, pp. 217–223; McGoldrick, M. "Ethnicity and Family Therapy: An Overview," in McGoldrick, Pearce, J., and Giordano, J., eds., *Ethnicity and Family Therapy*, New York: Guilford Press, 1984, p. 21; and Sue, D. *Counseling the Culturally Different*. New York: John Wiley & Sons, 1981, pp. 66–68.

10. For a poignant evaluation of cultural attitudes toward women, see James, M., "The Down-Scripting of Women for 115 Generations: A Historic Kaleidoscope," *Transactional Analysis Journal*, Vol. 3, No. 1, January 1973, pp. 15–22. See also Markus, H., et al., "Self-Schemas and Gender," *Journal of Personality and Social Psychology*, 1982, Vol. 42, pp. 38–50.

11. Cohen, C., "Goals and Schemata in Person Perception: Making Sense from the Stream of Behavior," in Cantor, N. and Kihlstrom, J., Eds., *Cognition, Social Interaction and Personality*, Hillsdale, N.J.: Erlbaum, 1982; Swann, W., and Read, S., "Acquiring Self-Knowledge: The Search for Feedback That Fits," *Journal of Personality and Social Psychology*, 1981, Vol. 41, pp. 1119–1128; Anderson, C., Lepper, M., and Ross, L., "Perseverance of Social Theories: The Role of Explanation in the Persistence of Discredited Information," *Journal of Personality and Social Psychology*, 1980, Vol. 39, pp. 1037–1049; Lord, C., Ross, L., and Lepper, M., "Biased Assimilation and Attitude Polarization: The Effects of Prior Theories on Subsequently Considered Evidence," *Journal of Personality and Social Psychology*, 1979, Vol. 37, pp. 2098–2109; Bargh, J., "Attention and Automaticity in the Processing of Self-Relevant

Information," *Journal of Personality and Social Psychology*, 1982, Vol. 43, pp. 425–436; Sagar, H., and Schofield, J., "Racial and Behavioral Cues in Black and White Children's Perceptions of Ambiguously Aggressive Acts," *Journal of Personality and Social Psychology*, 1980, Vol. 39, pp. 590–598.

12. For more on the power and techniques of visualization, see Garfield, C., *Peak Performance: Mental Training Techniques for the World's Greatest Athletes*, Los Angeles: Jeremy Tarcher, 1984; McKim, R., *Experiences in Visual Thinking*, Belmont, Calif.: Wadsworth Publishing, 1972. For more on positive affirmations, see Ray, S., *I Deserve Love: How Affirmations Can Guide You to Personal Fulfillment*, Berkeley, Calif.: Celestial Arts, 1976; and James, M., *It's Never Too Late to Be Happy*, Reading, Mass.: Addison-Wesley, 1985.

13. Russianoff, P., *Why Do I Think I'm Nothing Without a Man?* New York: Bantam Books, 1983, p. 43. Edwards and Hoover refer to this phenomenon as "the panic-to-pair" in Edwards, M. and Hoover, E., *The Challenge of Being Single*, New York: New American Library, 1974, p. 23.

14. Bennett, N., Craig, P. and Bloom, D., "Marriage Patterns in the United States," in *Newsweek*, June 2, 1986, pp. 54–61. In that article, sociologist Nancy Chodorow claims that "when you look at men who don't marry, you're often looking at the bottom of the barrel, . . . but when you look at the women who don't marry, you're looking at the cream of the crop." The pessimism of this research has been challenged by numerous authors, including Rozen, L., "The Great American Man Shortage: Whatta Lie," *Mademoiselle*, September 1986, pp. 246 ff.

15. See Jung, C., *Modern Man in Search of a Soul*, New York: Harcourt, Brace and Co., 1933; Von Franz, M., *Shadow and Evil in Fairy Tales*, Dallas: Spring Publications, 1983; the "disowned self" dealt with by Perls, F., et al., *Gestalt Therapy*, New York: Dell Publishing, 1951, pp. 146–189; and the "not-me" of Sullivan, H., *The Interpersonal Theory of Psychiatry*, New York: Norton, 1953, pp. 161–164.

16. For more on time concepts as a determinant of behavior, see Berne, E., *Sex in Human Loving*, New York: Simon & Schuster, 1970, pp. 166–171; Berne, E., *What Do You Do After You Say Hello*, New York: Grove Press, 1972, pp. 205–212; and Woollams, S. and Brown, M., *Transactional Analysis*, Dexter, Mich.: Huron Valley Institute, 1978, pp. 225–238.

17. See Asch, S., "Forming Impressions of Personality," *Journal of Abnormal and Social Psychology*, 1946, Vol. 41, pp. 258–290; Fiske, S., "Attention and Weight in Person Perception: The Impact of Negative and Extreme Behavior," *Journal of Personality and Social Psychology*, 1980, Vol. 38, pp. 889–906; Garwood, S., et al., "Beauty Is Only 'Name' Deep:

The Effect of First-Names in Ratings of Physical Attraction," *Journal of Applied Psychology*, 1980, Vol. 19, pp. 431–435; Gouaux, C., "Induced Affective States and Interpersonal Attraction," *Journal of Personality and Social Psychology*, 1971, Vol. 20, pp. 37–43; Griffitt, W., "Environmental Effects on Interpersonal Affective Behavior: Ambient Effective Temperature and Attraction," *Journal of Personality and Social Psychology*, 1970, Vol. 15, pp. 240–244; Kaplan, M., "Measurement and Generality of Response Dispositions in Person Perception," *Journal of Personality*, 1976, Vol. 44, pp. 179–194; Veithch, R., and Griffitt, W., "Good News, Bad News: Affective and Interpersonal Effects," *Journal of Applied Social Psychology*, 1976, Vol. 6, pp. 69–75.

18. Brigham, J., "Limiting Conditions of the Physical Attractiveness Stereotype: Attributions About Divorce," *Journal of Research in Personality*, 1980, Vol. 14, pp. 365–375. See also Gillen, B., "Physical Attractiveness: A Determinant of Two Types of Goodness," *Personality and Social Psychology Bulletin*, 1981, Vol. 7, pp. 277–281.

19. Harrison, A., and Saeed, L., "Let's Make a Deal: An Analysis of Revelations and Stipulations in Lonely Hearts and Advertisements," *Journal of Personality and Social Psychology*, 1977, Vol. 35, pp. 257–264.

20. Salholz, E., et al., "Too Late for Prince Charming," *Newsweek*, June 2, 1986, p. 61; Kantrowitz, B., et al., "The New Mating Games," *Newsweek*, June 2, 1986, p. 58.

21. For more on games, see Berne, E., *Games People Play*, New York: Grove Press, 1964; James, J., "The Game Plan," *Transactional Analysis Journal*, Vol. 3, No. 4, October 1973, pp. 14–17; James, J., and James, M., "Games Parents Play," in Arnold, E., ed., *Helping Parents Help Their Children*, New York: Brunner Mazel, 1978, pp. 65–82.

22. For more on this, see James, J., "Positive Payoffs After Games," *Transactional Analysis Journal*, Vol. 6, No. 3, July, 1976, pp. 259–262.

23. See Berne, E., *Transactional Analysis in Psychotherapy*, New York: Grove Press, 1961; and James, M., and Jongeward, D., *Born to Win*, Reading, Mass.: Addison-Wesley, 1971.

24. Palmer, G., "Social Currencies," *Transactional Analysis Journal*, 1977, Vol. 7, No. 1, pp. 20–23.

25. Ortega y Gassett, J., *On Love*, Cleveland: World Publishing, 1961, p. 51.

26. Bernstein, M., and Crosby, F., "An Empirical Examination of Relative Deprivation Theory," *Journal of Experimental Social Psychology*, 1980, 16, pp. 442–456; Berschied, E., and Walster, E., "A Little Bit About Love," in Houston, T., ed., *Foundations of Interpersonal*

Attraction, New York: Academic Press, 1974; and Dion, K. K. and Dion, K. L., "Self-Esteem and Romantic Love," *Journal of Personality*, 1975, 43, pp. 39–57.

27. Tesser, A., and Paulhus, D., "Toward a Causal Model of Love," *Journal of Personality and Social Psychology*, 1976, 34, pp. 1095–1105.

28. Averill, J., and Boothroyd, P., "On Falling in Love in Conformance with the Romantic Ideal," *Motivation and Emotion*, 1977, 1, pp. 235–247. Rubin, Peplau, and Hill concluded that whereas men seem to fall in love at first sight more frequently than women, women take more time to fall in love and they are the first to fall out of love and to end the relationship. Rubin, Z., Peplau, L., and Hill, C., "Loving and Leaving: Sex Differences in Attachments," *Sex Roles*, 1981, Vol. 7, pp. 821–835.

29. Leonard, J., "Private Lives," *New York Times*, February 13, 1980, p. C16; and Vernon, J., "Is It Love or Total Addiction?" *Feeling Great*, July 1985, p. 62.

30. Buber, M., *The Way of Man*, New York: Citadel Press, 1950, p. 29. Psychologist Sidney Jourard put it, "We are all role players, every one of us. We say that we feel things we do not feel. We say that we did things we did not do. We say that we believe things we do not believe. We pretend that we are loving when we are full of hostility. We pretend that we are calm and indifferent when we actually are trembling with anxiety and fear." Jourard, S., "The Fear That Cheats Us of Love," *Redbook*, October 1971, p. 83. See also Jourard, S., *The Transparent Self*, New York: Van Nostrand, 1964, and Jourard, S., *Disclosing Man to Himself*, New York: Van Nostrand, 1968.

31. Winstanley, R., as reported by Meer, J., "Happy Days for Executives' Wives," *Psychology Today*, February 1985, p. 80.

32. See Berne, E., *What Do You Do After You Say Hello*, New York: Grove Press, 1972, pp. 139–147. See also the concept of "gunny sacking" in Bach, G., and Wyden, P., *The Intimate Enemy: How to Fight Fair in Love and Marriage*, New York: Avon Books, 1981, pp. 16, 60.

33. Klagsbrun, F., *Married People: Staying Together in the Age of Divorce*, New York: Bantam, 1985; and Hales, D., "10 Secrets of a Happy Marriage," *McCall's*, February 1986, p. 154.

34. For more on fair fighting principles, see Bach, G., and Wyden, P., *The Intimate Enemy: How to Fight Fair in Love and Marriage*, New York: Avon Books, 1981. See also Campbell, S., *Beyond the Power Struggle*, San Luis Obispo, Calif.: Impact Publishers, 1984; Gottman, J., et al., *A Couple's Guide to Communication*, New York: Research Press, 1976; Gorkin, M., "Anger or Aggression: Confronting the Passionate Edge," *Legal Assistant Today*, Winter 1986, pp. 21–30.

35. Lauer, J., and Lauer, R., "Marriages Made to Last," *Psychology Today*, June 1985, p. 26.

36. Theorists and clinicians have espoused many theories of what makes marriage last. Their opinions have been primarily based on both logic and clinical experience. Recently these clinical observations have been supported by reliable statistical research. See Lauer, J., and Lauer, R., "Marriages Made to Last," *Psychology Today*, June 1985, pp. 22–26; Gottman, J., *Marital Interactions: Experimental Investigations*, New York: Academic Press, 1979; Levinger, G., in Raush, G., and Raush, H., *Close Relationships: Perspectives on the Meaning of Intimacy*, Amherst, Mass.: University of Massachusetts Press, 1977; and several research studies reviewed by Hales, D., "10 Secrets of a Happy Marriage," *McCall's*, February 1986. See also Howard, J., *Families*, New York: Simon and Schuster, 1978, for qualities happy families have in common.

37. See Beal, E., "Separation, Divorce, and Single-Parent Families," in Carter, E., and McGoldrick, M., eds., *The Family Life Cycle: A Framework for Family Therapy*, New York: Gardner Press, 1980, pp. 241–264; Gelman, D., et al., "Playing Both Mother and Father," *Newsweek*, July 15, 1985, pp. 42–50; Robinson, B., and Barret, R., "Teenage Fathers," *Psychology Today*, December 1985, pp. 66–70.

38. See Baxter, L., and Wilmot, W., "Secret Tests: Social Strategies for Acquiring Information About the State of the Relationship," *Human Communications Research*, Winter 1984, Vol. 11, No. 2, pp. 171–201; White, G., "Inducing Jealousy: A Power Perspective," *Personality and Social Psychology Bulletin*, 1980, Vol. 6, pp. 222–227; White, G., "Model of Romantic Jealousy," *Motivation and Emotion*, 1981, Vol. 5, pp. 295–310.

39. See Friedman, M., *Martin Buber: The Life of Dialogue*, New York: Harper, 1960, pp. 57–100; and James, M., *Born to Love*, Reading, Mass.: Addison-Wesley, 1975, pp. 188–190.

40. Buber, M. *Between Man and Man*. Boston: Beacon Press, 1955, p. 35.

41. Kernberg, O., in Kwitney, Z., "The Many-Splendored Stages of a Relationship," *Cosmopolitan*, April 1985, pp. 227–231.

42. de Beauvoir, S., *The Second Sex*, New York: Knopf, 1953.

43. Bennis, W., and Nanus, B., *Leaders: The Strategies for Taking Charge*, New York: Harper & Row, 1985, pp. 61ff.

Bibliography

Allport, Gordon. *Becoming*. New Haven: Yale University Press, 1955.

Andersen, S., and Bem, S. "Sex Typing and Androgyny in Dyadic Interaction: Individual Differences in Responsiveness to Physical Attractiveness," *Journal of Personality and Social Psychology*, 1981, Vol. 41, pp. 74–86.

Anderson, C., Lepper, M., and Ross, L. "Perseverance of Social Theories: The Role of Explanation in the Persistence of Discredited Information," *Journal of Personality and Social Psychology*, 1980, Vol. 39, pp. 1037–1049.

Arnold, L. Eugene, ed. *Helping Parents Help Their Children*. New York: Brunner/Mazel, 1978.

Asch, S. "Forming Impressions of Personality," *Journal of Abnormal and Social Psychology*, 1946, Vol. 41, pp. 258–290.

Averill, J., and Boothroyd, P. "On Falling in Love in Conformance with the Romantic Ideal," *Motivation and Emotion*, 1977, Vol. 1, pp. 235–247.

Bach, G., and Wyden, P. *The Intimate Enemy: How to Fight Fair in Love and Marriage*. New York: Avon Books, 1981.

Bargh, J. "Attention and Automaticity in the Processing of Self-Relevant Information," *Journal of Personality and Social Psychology*, 1982, Vol. 43, pp. 425–436.

Baxter, L., and Wilmot, W. "Secret Tests: Social Strategies for Acquiring Information about the State of the Relationship," *Human Communications Research*, Winter 1984, Vol. 11, No. 2, pp. 171–201.

Beck, Aaron. *Depression: Causes and Treatment*. Philadelphia: University of Pennsylvania Press, 1970.

Bennett, N., Craig, P., and Bloom, D. "Marriage Patterns in the United States," *Newsweek*, June 2, 1986, pp. 54–61.

Bennis, Warren, and Nanus, Burt. *Leaders: The Strategies for Taking Charge*. New York: Harper and Row, 1985.

Berne, Eric. *What Do You Do After You Say Hello?* New York: Grove Press, 1972.

———. *Sex in Human Loving.* New York: Simon and Schuster, 1970.

———. *Games People Play.* New York: Grove Press, 1964.

———. *Transactional Analysis in Psychotherapy.* New York: Grove Press, 1961.

Bernstein, M., and Crosby, F. "An Empirical Examination of Relative Deprivation Theory," *Journal of Experimental Social Psychology,* 1980, Vol. 16, pp. 442–456.

Boszormenyi-Nagy, I., and Krasner, B. "Trust-based Therapy: A Contextual Approach," *American Journal of Psychiatry,* 1980, Vol. 137, No. 7, pp. 767–775.

Boszormenyi-Nagy, I., and Spark, G. *Invisible Loyalties.* New York: Harper & Row, 1973.

Bower, G., et al. "Scripts in Memory for Text," *Cognitive Psychology,* 1979, Vol. 11, pp. 177–220.

Bridges, William. *Transitions: Making Sense of Life's Changes.* Reading, Mass.: Addison-Wesley, 1980.

Brigham, J. "Limiting Condition of the Physical Attractiveness Stereotype: Attributions about Divorce," *Journal of Research in Personality,* 1980, Vol. 14, pp. 365–375.

Buber, Martin. *Between Man and Man.* Boston: Beacon Press, 1955.

———. *The Way of Man.* New York: Citadel Press, 1950.

Cameron-Bandler, Leslie. *They Lived Happily Ever After.* Cupertino, Calif.: Meta Publications, 1978.

Campbell, Donald. "On the Conflicts Between Biological and Social Evolution and Between Psychology and Moral Tradition," *American Psychologist,* December 1975, pp. 1103–1125.

Campbell, Susan. *Beyond the Power Struggle.* San Luis Obispo, Calif.: Impact Publishers, 1984.

———. *The Couple's Journey.* San Luis Obispo, Calif.: Impact Publishers, 1980.

Cantor, N., and Kihlstrom, J., eds. *Cogition, Social Interaction and Personality.* Hillsdale, N.J.: Erlbaum, 1982.

Carter, E. and McGoldrick, M., eds. *The Family Life Cycle: A Framework for Family Therapy.* New York: Gardner Press, 1980.

Cowan, Connell, and Kinder, M. *Smart Women, Foolish Choices*. New York: Clarkson Potter, 1985.

Davis, Keith "Near and Dear: Friendship and Love Compared," *Psychology Today*, February 1985, pp. 22–30.

Davitz, Lois. "My Ideal Woman," *McCall's*, July 1985.

de Beauvoir, Simone. *The Second Sex*. New York: Knopf, 1953.

Dion, K. K., and Dion, K. L. "Self-Esteem and Romantic Love," *Journal of Personality*, 1976, Vol. 43, pp. 39–57.

Dowling, Colette. *The Cinderella Complex*. New York: Simon & Schuster, 1981.

Edwards, M., and Hoover, E. *The Challenge of Being Single*. New York: New American Library, 1974.

Erikson, Erik. *Childhood and Society*. New York: Norton, 1963.

Ferrucci, Piero. *What We May Be*. Los Angeles: Tarcher, 1982.

Fiske, S., and Taylor, S. *Social Cognition*. Reading, Mass.: Addison-Wesley, 1983, pp. 543–557.

Fiske, S. "Attention and Weight in Person Perception: The Impact of Negative and Extreme Behavior," *Journal of Personality and Social Psychology*, 1980, Vol. 38, pp. 889–906.

Frankl, Viktor. *The Doctor and the Soul*. New York: Bantam Books, 1967.

————. *Man's Search for Meaning*. New York: Washington Square Press, 1965.

Friedman, Maurice, ed. *The Worlds of Existentialism: A Critical Reader*. New York: Random House, 1964.

Friedman, Maurice, *Martin Buber: The Life of Dialogue*. New York: Harper, 1960.

Garfield, Charles. *Peak Performance: Mental Training Techniques for the World's Greatest Athletes*. Los Angeles: Jeremy Tarcher, 1984.

————. *Peak Performers: The New Heroes of American Business*. New York: Morrow, 1986.

Garwood, S., et al. "Beauty Is Only 'Name' Deep: The Effect of First-Names in Ratings of Physical Attraction," *Journal of Applied Psychology*, 1980, Vol. 19, pp. 431–435.

Gaylin, Willard. *Feelings*. New York: Ballantine, 1979.

Gelman, David, et al. "Playing Both Mother and Father," *Newsweek*, July 15, 1985, pp. 42–50.

Gillen, B. "Physical Attractiveness: A Determinant of Two Types of Goodness," *Personality and Social Psychology Bulletin*, 1981, Vol. 7, pp. 277–281.

Gilligan, Carol. *In a Different Voice*. Cambridge: Harvard University Press, 1982.

Gorkin, M. "Anger or Aggression: Confronting the Passionate Edge," *Legal Assistant Today*, Winter 1986, pp. 21–30.

Gottman, John. *Marital Interactions: Experimental Investigations*. New York: Academic Press, 1979.

Gottman, John, et al. *A Couple's Guide to Communication*. New York: Research Press, 1976.

Gouaux, C. "Induced Affective States and Interpersonal Attraction," *Journal of Personality and Social Psychology*, 1971, Vol. 20, pp. 37–43.

Griffitt, W. "Environmental Effects on Interpersonal Affective Behavior: Ambient Effective Temperature and Attraction," *Journal of Personality and Social Psychology*, 1970, Vol. 44, pp. 179–194.

Goulding, Mary, and Goulding, Robert. *Changing Lives Through Redecision Therapy*. New York: Brunner/Mazel, 1979.

———. *The Power is in the Patient*. San Francisco: TA Press, 1978.

Hales, Diane. "10 Secrets of a Happy Marriage," *McCall's*, February 1986, p. 154.

Harrison, A., and Saeed, L. "Let's Make a Deal: An Analysis of Revelations and Stipulations in Lonely Hearts and Advertisements," *Journal of Personality and Social Psychology*, 1977, Vol. 35, pp. 257–264.

Hastie, R., and Kumar, P. "Person Memory: Personality Traits as Organizing Principles in Memory for Behavior," *Journal of Personality and Social Psychology*, 1979, Vol. 37, pp. 25–38.

Higgins, E., Herman, C., and Zanna, M., eds. *Social Cognition*. Hillsdale, N.J.: Erlbaum, 1981.

Houston, T., ed. *Foundations of Interpersonal Attraction*, New York: Academic Press, 1974.

Howard, Jane. *Families*. New York: Simon & Schuster, 1978.

Huizinga, John. *Homo Ludens: A Study of the Play Element in Culture*. Boston: Beacon Press, 1950.

James, John. "Grandparents and the Family Script Parade," *Transactional Analysis Journal*, January 1984, Vol. 14, No. 1, pp. 18–28.

―――. "Cultural Consciousness: The Challenge to T.A.," *Transactional Analysis Journal*, Vol. 13, No. 4, October 1983, pp. 207–216.

―――. "Positive Payoffs After Games," *Transactional Analysis Journal*, Vol. 6, No. 3, July 1976, pp. 259–262.

―――. "The Game Plan," *Transactional Analysis Journal*, Vol. 3, No. 4, October 1973, pp. 14–17.

James, Muriel. *It's Never Too Late to Be Happy.* Reading, Mass.: Addison-Wesley, 1985.

―――. *Marriage is for Loving.* Reading, Mass.: Addison-Wesley, 1979.

―――. *Born to Love.* Reading, Mass.: Addison-Wesley, 1975.

―――. "The Down-Scripting of Women for 115 Generations: A Historic Kaleidoscope," *Transactional Analysis Journal*, Vol. 3, No. 1, January 1973, pp. 15–22.

James, Muriel, and Jongeward, Dorothy. *Born to Win.* Reading, Mass.: Addison-Wesley, 1971.

Jourard, Sidney. "The Fear That Cheats Us of Love," *Redbook*, October 1971, p. 83.

―――. *Disclosing Man to Himself.* New York: Van Nostrand, 1968.

―――. *The Transparent Self.* New York: Van Nostrand, 1964.

Jung, Carl. *Modern Man in Search of a Soul.* New York: Harcourt, Brace and Co., 1933.

Kantrowitz, Barbara, et al. "The New Mating Games," *Newsweek*, June 2, 1986, p. 58.

Kaplan, M. "Measurement and Generality of Response Dispositions in Person Perception," *Journal of Personality*, 1976, Vol. 44, pp. 179–194.

Kent, Corita, and Pintaro, John. *To Believe in Man.* New York: Harper & Row, 1970.

Keesing, R. "Paradigms Lost: The New Ethnography and the New Linguistics," *Southwestern Journal of Anthropology*, 1972, Vol. 28, pp. 299–332.

―――. "Theories of Culture," *Annual Reviews of Anthropology,* Palo Alto, Calif.: Annual Reviews Inc., 1974, pp. 73–98.

Kiley, Dan. *The Peter Pan Syndrome.* New York: Avon, 1983.

Klagsbrun, Francine. *Married People: Staying Together in the Age of Divorce*. New York: Bantam, 1985.

Kwitney, Ziva. "The Many-Splendored Stages of a Relationship," *Cosmopolitan*, April 1985, pp. 227–231.

Lauer, Jeanette, and Lauer, Robert. "Marriages Made to Last," *Psychology Today*, June 1985, pp. 22–26.

Leonard, J. "Private Lives," *New York Times*, February 13, 1980, p. C16.

Leslie, Robert. *Jesus and Logotherapy*. Nashville: Abingdon Press, 1965.

Levinson, Daniel, et al. *The Seasons of a Man's Life*. New York: Ballantine Books, 1978.

Lord, C., Ross, L., and Lepper, M. "Biases Assimilation and Attitude Polarization: The Effects of Prior Theories on Subsequently Considered Evidence," *Journal of Personality and Social Psychology*, 1979, Vol. 37, pp. 2098–2109.

Markus, H., et al. "Self-Schemas and Gender," *Journal of Personality and Social Psychology*, 1982, Vol. 42, pp. 38–50.

Maslow, Abraham. *The Psychology of Being*. New York: Van Nostrand, 1962.

May, Rollo. *The Courage to Create*. New York: Bantam Books, 1976.

McGoldrick, Monica, et al. *Ethnicity and Family Therapy*. New York: Guilford Press, 1984.

McKim, R. *Experiences in Visual Thinking*. Belmont, Calif.: Celestial Arts, 1976.

Meer, Jeff. "Happy Days for Executives' Wives," *Psychology Today*, February 1985, p. 80.

Mitchell, Arnold. *The Nine American Lifestyles*. New York: Warner Books, 1984.

Moreland, R., and Zajonc, R. "Exposure Effects in Person Perception: Familiarity, Similarity, and Attraction," *Journal of Experimental Social Psychology*, 1982, p. 18.

Norwood, Robin. *Women Who Love Too Much*. New York: Tarcher, 1985.

Ortega y Gasset, Jose. *On Love*. Cleveland: World Publishing, 1961.

Palmer, Gaylon. "Social Currencies," *Transactional Analysis Journal*, 1977, Vol. 7, No. 1, pp. 20–23.

Peck, M. Scott. *The Road Less Traveled*. New York: Simon & Schuster, 1978.

Peele, Stanton. *Love and Addiction*. New York: New American Library, 1975.

Perls, Fritz, et al. *Gestalt Therapy*. New York: Dell Publishing, 1951.

Raush, G., and Raush, H. *Close Relationships: Perspectives on the Meaning of Intimacy*. Amherst, Mass.: University of Massachusetts Press, 1977.

Ray, Sandra. *I Deserve Love: How Affirmations Can Guide You To Personal Fulfillment*. Berkeley, Calif.: Celestial Arts, 1976.

Robinson, B., and Barret, R. "Teenage Fathers," *Psychology Today*, December 1985, pp. 66–70.

Rozen, Leah. "The Great American Man Shortage: Whatta Lie," *Mademoiselle*, September 1986, pp. 246ff.

Rubin, Z., Peplau, L., and Hill, C. "Loving and Leaving: Sex Differences in Attachments," *Sex Roles*, 1981, Vol. 7, pp. 821–835.

Ruppel, H. "Religiosity and Premarital Sexual Permissiveness," *Journal of Marriage and the Family*, 1970, Vol. 32, No. 4, pp. 647–655.

Russianoff, Penelope. *Why Do I Think I'm Nothing Without A Man?* New York: Bantam Books, 1983.

Sagar, H., and Schofield, J. "Racial and Behavioral Cues in Black and White Children's Perceptions of Ambiguously Aggressive Acts," *Journal of Personality and Social Psychology*, 1980, Vol. 39, pp. 590–598.

Salholz, E., et al. "Too Late for Prince Charming," *Newsweek*, June 2, 1986, p. 61.

Satir, Virginia. *Peoplemaking*. Palo Alto, Calif.: Science and Behavior Books, 1972.

Selye, Hans. *Stress Without Distress*. New York: New American Library, 1975.

———. *The Stress of Life*. New York: McGraw-Hill, 1978.

Sheehy, Gail. *Passages: Predictable Crises in Adult Life*. New York: E. P. Dutton, 1976.

Spanier, G. "Sexualization and Premarital Sexual Behavior," *The Family Coordinator*, 1975, Vol. 24, No. 1, pp. 33–41.

Sue, Derald. *Counseling the Culturally Different*. New York: Wiley, 1981.

Sullivan, Harry Stack. *The Interpersonal Theory of Psychiatry*. New York: Norton, 1953.

Swann, W., and Read, S. "Acquiring Self-Knowledge: The Search for Feedback that Fits," *Journal of Personality and Social Psychology*, 1981, Vol. 41, pp. 1119–1128.

Tesser, A., and Paulhaus, D. "Toward a Causal Model of Love," *Journal of Personality and Social Psychology*, 1976, Vol. 34, pp. 1095–1105.

Veithch, R., and Griffitt, W. "Good News, Bad News: Affective and Interpersonal Effects," *Journal of Applied Social Psychology*, 1976, Vol. 6, pp. 69–75.

Vernon, J. "Is It Love or Total Addiction?" *Feeling Great*, July 1985, p. 62.

Von Franz, Marie-Louise. *Shadow and Evil in Fairy Tales*. Dallas: Spring Publications, 1983.

Wakil, S., "Campus Mate Selection Preferences: A Cross-Cultural Comparison," *Social Forces*, 1973, Vol. 53, pp. 471–476.

Walster, Elaine, and Walster, G. William. *A New Look at Love*. Reading, Mass.: Addison-Wesley, 1978.

Walters, Lynda. "How Habits Strain Marriage," *Medical Aspects of Human Sexuality*, August 1982, Vol. 16, No. 8, pp. 48ff.

Welwood, John. *Challenge of the Heart: Love, Sex and Intimacy in Changing Times*. Boston: Shambhala, 1985.

White, G. "Model of Romantic Jealousy," *Motivation and Emotion*, 1981, Vol. 5, pp. 295–310.

Woollams, Stan and Brown, Mike. *Transactional Analysis*. Dexter, Mich.: Huron Valley Institute, 1978.

Note to Readers

We want to hear from you! We want to hear about your success stories—how you met that someone special and discovered that you were right for each other. We'd like to know how our ideas and techniques helped you. We also encourage you to send us your ideas and suggestions so that we can continue to share them, along with tips, advice, and information, with others—in our speeches, seminars, and workshops which we present across America and internationally. If you are interested in learning more about these programs or having us come to your area, please write to us.

We wish you the best!

John James and Ibis Schlesinger
P.O. Box 356
Lafayette, CA 94549

Index